HOW TO USE YOUR TIME
TO GET THINGS DONE

HOW TO
USE YOUR TIME
TO GET
THINGS DONE

by
Edwin B. Feldman, P.E.

Frederick Fell Publishers, Inc.

New York

TO ZEL
WHO MAKES EVERYTHING POSSIBLE

CONTENTS

INTRODUCTION

WHAT THIS BOOK WILL DO FOR YOU

I know you—we've met many times before. Yes, of course, you are the one on his way up. You seem to get around a good deal. I have seen you discussing, reading, listening, working hard—but I see you have developed a frown.

I think I know what's troubling you: you feel that there is simply not enough time to get things done—you've used it all up. You're worried that somehow the days keep on going by and you're just not able to do the things you want to do and need to do.

Perhaps it seems hopeless to you. But it really isn't, not at all. This matter of the utilization of time can be handled methodically. You can put time to work for you, or you can serve the clock as an automaton would serve a machine. The choice is entirely yours.

Yes, there are some prerequisites, but knowing you as I do, I believe you will provide them.

All accomplishment—other than that which is the result of accident—undergoes three stages:

1. The goal
2. The plan
3. The action

This goal—plan—action sequence isn't always conscious: we may have unconscious goals. But we mustn't make the mistake of skipping one of the steps or changing the order, as is so often done. You can catch yourself every day taking action on a goal you have set without having developed a plan, or setting a goal and making a plan without ever taking action, or even taking action without reference to either a goal or a plan.

This book, then, has been developed to help you toward greater accomplishment through time control by using that same G-P-A sequence (that, understandably, so resembles the Scientific Method). The effective use of your time can be more simple than you may think, but it can never be *mechanical*. It isn't a matter of plugging numbers into formulas. So, you will find that the opening chapters of this book will help you with this business of setting goals and making plans.

Use the systems and techniques you will find in this book. They are readily identified and can be put to work for you in a step-by-step fashion, without confusion.

Work hard at them—give yourself a year. You will develop a number of new habits and discard some old ones. I predict that the results will surprise you! You will find that you are able to get many more things done in a more effective way, not by stealing from Peter to pay Paul, not at the expense of time for your family, hobbies, recreation. You will end a day's work feeling better about what you have been able to accomplish, and you will look forward to the next day's work without concern.

And these techniques will do one thing more. They will help you answer a very important question: *why*. An inconclusive answer to that question, for many of us, locks doors that may never be opened.

If we are intelligent, we profit from our own mistakes, but, if we should be *wise*, we must learn from the mistakes of others. Later chapters post warning signs for us so we can be on the lookout for, and thus avoid, the hazards to time saving that so many people become lost in.

Succeeding chapters will give you the actual tools for the job—proven techniques and ideas you can put to work *tomorrow morning*, either selectively or as a whole program. These systems are not just theory; they are workable, practical ideas that are used by our clients every day.

They can help *you* every day.

Let's imagine, through a coincidence that really would not be too far-fetched, that a "manned" space ship from Venus were to land on earth at just about the same time that one of our own space ships landed there.

If contact were made without both parties killing each other through fear or malice, a feverish attempt would be made to establish a system of *communication*, because each group would have a burning desire to ask the other civilization these fundamental questions:

What is the meaning of life?
Is the universe infinite?
Who (or what) is God?
How can peoples live together in peace?
Is there an after-life?
What is time and how should we use it?

The uses of time is not a problem for a few selected people at various periods, but unquestionably is a *universal* problem.

The principal difference between you and a cadaver of your same age, sex and size in the morgue is the fact that he has run out of time and you have not. Your future will be determined principally by how you use your time: the goals you set, the plans you make, the action you take. It's a matter of application.

You've gotten this far, so you already have provided the first requirement: you have shown interest. Shall we go on?

1

YOU *CAN* GET MORE DONE!

Do not think that what is hard for thee to master is impossible for man; but if a thing is possible and proper to man, deem it attainable by thee.

—MARCUS AURELIUS

A STRANGE BOARD MEETING

Two board members were on their feet, and the chairman was wondering how to handle it all.

Tom Carson stood there with his mouth open, stopped in the middle of a sentence.

No wonder; anyone would have been shocked at what Joe Barry had just done. Contrary to all protocol (and no doubt, even good manners), he had wearily stood up, shaking his head, and interrupted Carson's presentation.

The board meeting had been in progress for some time. Barry wasn't even an officer of the company, just a consultant. To most people, the meeting would have appeared to be going very smoothly. Each executive gave his report of past performance, present activities and proposed plans, with the chairman moderating the discussion. But there Barry was, a man known to be quiet and reserved, on his feet, out of order and disrupting a board meeting.

"Gentlemen," Barry pleaded, "how can we manage our own affairs, and direct the activities of the other persons in this corporation, unless we are able to control the use of our *own* time! My apologies to Mr. Carson, and to you, Mr. Chairman, but my patience just ran out. It was a question of having an instant ulcer through sheer frustration or of speaking up—and I don't believe in ulcers!"

Grimes, the chairman, undecided what to do, had the gavel poised. Barry well knew that one of the advantages of being reserved under most conditions is that any raising of the voice, or unusual action, creates as much attention as would a firecracker. It's all a matter of contrast, of course.

Having boiled over, Barry was now simmering down. He addressed his remarks directly to the chairman now, rather more quietly. "Sir, ten men have been in this room an hour and a half now, and about an hour of that time has been wasted while we listened to the development of information that either should have been distributed before this meeting or should have been on the chalkboard when we walked in. So far, we've wasted ten man-hours of the most precious commodity this company has—its executive talent."

Grimes didn't call him to order. Barry realized that Grimes must have been thinking the same thing. Carson was still standing, although, by now, his mouth was closed.

Barry looked at all the faces in turn—never had he received more rapt attention from them. He had touched a nerve. Now was no time to stop.

"What really concerns me, much more than this board meeting or even all the board meetings to come," he went on, "is the fact that I suspect the conduct of this company's executive work, on a day-to-day basis, is along these same unproductive lines."

A perfect silence fell.

"And what do you suggest?" finally asked Carson, naturally somewhat indignant.

The critic looked toward the chairman; Grimes was waiting for an answer to the question, and he nodded in acquiescence.

Barry went on. "Let me again apologize to you, Tom, by saying that my remarks are directed to the Board in general, as all are equally involved. Really, my feeling is that the most urgent business of this Board is to encourage each of its members—whether in sales, production, research, finance or what have you—to work hard and fast on the conservation and use of his own time, in order to achieve the company's objectives. It's difficult to get excited about the growth prospects for *this* company, as compared to its competition, under *these* conditions."

It was as if a bomb had been exploded; now it was time to smooth things over a little.

"There is a tremendous amount of talent in this company—it's just a shame to see so much of it wasted. The conservation of time—that is, getting things done—is a skill that must be learned and applied, just like any other skill. I should really no more expect all of you to have developed this skill than I would expect you to be expert billiard players or linguists. Frankly, most board meetings are run just like this one, and most business executives do their work just as I imagine you do yours. But I expect more from you than just the average, just as I know you expect it of yourselves. And I know I'm justified in this belief, because I see you sitting there listening, believing, wanting to hear more, rather than shouting me down."

It was true.

Carson was seated now. Grimes asked, "What would you suggest we do, Mr. Barry?" The question was a real one; he was too big a man to be sarcastic.

Joe Barry shoved his chair back and slowly walked up to the big chalkboard. By the time he was ready to write, he had had a little time to organize some thoughts.

"First, gentlemen," he began, "I'm in the same boat as you are. I get angrier with myself more than you think I have gotten with you, because I *know* the rules and have seen them work, yet I find *myself* failing to use them. Yes, believe me, we're all in the same boat together.

"There are some basic rules for getting things done," he continued. "You can't afford to break or bend more than a few of them if you intend to be truly effective in your work."

He began writing. In fifteen minutes he listed about fifteen items, starting with the recognition of the value of time and the identification of basic objectives. Pretty soon, other members of the group were not only anticipating items on the list but also elaborating and giving examples from their own experience. Some copied the list down item for item. Barry had attended previous meetings concerning such stimulating subjects as mergers, new product development, election of officers, but never had he seen so intense an interest as was being shown in that list.

Finally, after he had completed and discussed his list, he sat down, feeling he had done something worthwhile though only scratching the surface.

From time to time, after the meeting, those same board members would tell him, sometimes surprised but always excited, about how much time they had saved by just concentrating on one or two items on that list. The research director, for example, told how he had cut his time for personal interviews in half by remaining standing on greeting the caller, taking a seat along with his visitor only where a subject of exceptional value to the company was brought up. Many thousands of dollars in additional profits have come to that company by his being able to spend another hour every day in directing their research efforts.

But it was a drop in the bucket. The proper utilization of time by a company's executives can be achieved only through a comprehensive program of time conservation, even though each step is relatively simple. The random use of one or two good ideas would no more transform Grimes' company than any of the managers and supervisors in it, even though identifiable benefits would be enjoyed.

TIME, THE LOADED PISTOL

A marksman holding a pistol at a firing range, a cabinet maker working with razor-sharp chisels, a demolitions man fusing a plastic explosive, a Marine sergeant pulling the pin on a hand grenade at an obstacle course will all agree that for your own benefit you should not fear the hazard but develop a respect for it.

Time, then, is like a loaded pistol—not to be feared but to be respected.

The manager or supervisor who would do more needs to have a clear understanding of the economic value of time. Benjamin Franklin said that to love life is to love time, since time is the stuff that life is made of. Certainly, time is the stuff that business, commerce and industry are made of.

In reality, nothing has a value except in proportion to its time involvement. When you purchase a magazine at a news-stand, you are buying nothing more than hundreds of fragments of time which, added together, produced the saleable item and delivered it to the point of sale. The cost of the paper for the magazine involves the rental of land while timber grows to harvest, the labor to fell the timber and to build saws, the labor for transporting logs to the pulp mill, as well as for building the trucks to carry them there, the labor to build the mill and its equipment, to operate it, to provide the chemicals and water involved and to package and ship a finished paper. Principally, then, we are speaking of labor, and labor is always a function of time.

Nature doesn't charge us for the pine trees from which we make paper, nor for the earth, air, water and sunlight required by the trees; all the costs involve payment to men for their time.

Implied, then, in the question "How much does it cost?" is the equally valid question "How much time is it worth?"

The valuation put on an hour of time provided by a carpenter, a pilot, a lumberjack, an assembly worker or a policeman can be quickly and easily fixed. The same cannot be said of the executive. Oh yes, we can determine his salary, but that is *not* the true valuation of his time; it is worth much, much more.

Getting more done must involve an appreciation of management time; this will be discussed in detail in Chapter Two.

THE WILL TO DO

Someone once said that all you need to know about money is that if you've got it, you've got it; and if you ain't got it, you ain't got it. Perhaps the same thing could be said about the will to succeed: either one has it or he hasn't.

Perhaps you recognize in yourself this urge, this drive, to be somebody, to do something important, to be a success. If so, good; I can only hope that you have chosen the right direction for your energies. But it isn't always as simple as that. Many of our greatest leaders have a *quiet* determination, a drive that is not fed on sound and fury. Such a man may be a contender for your own job. Then, many important people have been "late bloomers," recognizing their own abilities and own need for self-expression only after years of relative quiescence.

Probably the capacity for drive must be in one from the beginning, but the expression of that will may require release.

Don't worry about whether or not you have this ability. If you are willing to do more than is merely required, then you have it at least to some degree. You won't be happy trying to fake such a drive, and that surely won't last long. The fact that you are reading books on self-improvement should be evidence, but not necessarily proof, that you are able to put this book to work for you. We will go into this further in Chapter Three.

PUTTING THE TOOLS TO WORK

As a consultant, I have been privileged to work with a number of industries and institutions in programming indirect labor requirements—those functions which are not directly involved in the production of the end product or service.

Here is a typical experience:

Manager: Now that you have recommended the desirable

organization, staffing and equipment, when can we change over to this system?

Consultant: Because of the new methods which will be used, involving unfamiliar materials and equipment, it is desirable first to conduct a training course.

Manager: As I told you before, we don't have time around here to conduct training classes on our regular time and no budget authorization for overtime. And you know darn well the men won't do it on their own time!

Consultant: We'll have to make time, Mr. Manager, by delaying some of the low-priority long-term projects. We can conduct training classes at the beginning of the work shift, and the men can put that information to use later in the day; we can follow up with on-the-job training later on in the day.

Manager: But what about bumping? That's another reason we've never held training classes. No sooner would we get a man trained, than he would go back into a production department.

Consultant: Your high turnover rate merely intensifies the need for training. Besides, the things these people will be learning will be beneficial to the company when they return to production—you'll be putting "maintenance missionaries" into the production departments!

There is an inescapable logic concerning training: no improvement can be made without change; change involves a transition of method, equipment, materials; a transition cannot be effected without an understanding of its means;

understanding requires learning; learning is provided by
teaching, which is training.

Not everyone needs a teacher, but the self-taught man
has to play the roles of both teacher and student.

A number of time-saving techniques will be identified
and discussed in the following chapters. Identification—
which can be done by a chimpanzee—is not enough. You
gain nothing from Mozart's *Forty-first Symphony* by identifying it as the *Jupiter*. Thus, it will not help you to know
that standing up helps you conserve time *unless* you understand the use of that tool and put it to work for you.

One of the fundamental principles of pedagogy (the
art of teaching) is that repetition is an indispensable part of
learning. This is particularly true with complex skills such
as self-management techniques. A good friend in Texas tells
me he is about two-thirds finished with Harry Lorayne's
How to Develop a Super-Power Memory. He has been
"reading" the book for three years—but of course most of
the time has been involved in putting Mr. Lorayne's memory system to work and practicing that system. This friend,
formerly afflicted with a poor memory, can now remember
a list of a hundred items. If he had merely read the book
and put it down, he would have benefited from the concepts
of "ridiculous association" and assigning names to numbers,
but surely he would not have developed the superb memory
he now has.

The same is true with this book, though not nearly to
the same extent. Getting more things done does not require
the memorization of a system and its practice hundreds of
times. But it does require a relentless use of the techniques
over a long enough period of time to make them habitual.

You can make progress merely by taking one or two
techniques and using them when convenient, but the transformation of your time-use habits will take a year.

Let me suggest a plan. As a preparation, on the basis of the first three chapters, do these three things:

1. Express in one or two sentences your basic personal objective or philosophy of life.
2. Evaluate the worth of your time—the time you save—for one minute, one hour, one day.
3. Develop a motto and post it where you will see it daily. For example, "I *will* get more done!"

Armed with these weapons, after you have read the entire book through, work on one chapter each month, beginning with Chapter Four. Spend that first month recognizing, identifying and avoiding indolence, diversion and procrastination. On the second month, go to the next chapter but also review the first. After several months, you may find the need to spend a full month on the accumulated material up to that time without taking on anything new.

You must be your own taskmaster, as any exceptionally productive person must be. Without this self-motivation, you must fall into that pool of hopelessness—of which the American public is so fond—known as "the average."

Wouldn't it be ironic if you fell into the trap of avoiding this issue by claiming that you did not have enough time to work at it!

EXTENDING YOUR CAPACITIES

It is one thing to save time and another to put it to the best possible use. To provide yourself the greatest possible return on the use of conserved time, it is desirable to broaden your scope and to stimulate your natural creative abilities.

None of us is fully developed. We have our limitations, our prejudices, our vacuums of information. Most people abandon the true creative spirit on leaving grade school, or before.

There are many things that you can do to develop your productive, managerial and creative abilities. Work on them; this activity is a natural companion to getting more done.

Do not be so rigid in your thinking as to limit your sources of understanding. Many companies spend a good deal of time and money just finding out what their competitors are doing. Learn from the man whom you think is most capable of taking your job. Learn from the man whose personal habits or appearance you do not like.

2

DO YOU REALLY WANT TO SAVE TIME?

It is a wretched taste to be gratified with mediocrity when the excellent lies before us.
—ISAAC D'ISRAELI

NOT EVERYONE WANTS TO SAVE TIME

Frank Johnson has just been promoted to vice-president of the Corday Fastener Company, let's say, and is at his desk considering what the future holds for him. His thoughts flit from one thing to another: increased income, more authority, the need for more information, personnel. But those thoughts always return to one thing—he's worried about how to find the time to make a success of the opportunity given him.

His problem: too little time.

Sitting in the same position, at the same time, is John Franklin. But Franklin is a hobo, and his legs are hanging out the doors of a Union Pacific box car, leaving Denver, for—who cares? Even a hobo needs a few dollars every now and then, and the harvesting season will start in a few weeks on the West Coast—an easy place to do a few days' light work and walk away when you've got enough money to last a while. But he'll have to knock around a few days more until it starts, and the money is all gone.

His problem: too much time.

Of course not everyone wants to save time. Between those who want to conserve as much time as possible, and those who want to expend as much as they can, is a complete spectrum of people who want to save time *to a certain extent.*

Aside from personal feelings, putting deadlines on some things can kill them. If Darwin had decided to publish his *Origin of Species* after one year of work, we probably never would have heard of it or him. It doesn't take an art connoisseur to evaluate some of the mass-production paintings now available by the gross. Some people in a research laboratory can be safely given deadlines—but then, some can't. Ralph McGill can write a great editorial every day, but another Atlantan, Margaret Mitchell, took a literary lifetime to write *Gone With the Wind.*

The value you will be able to obtain from this book, and any other effort at improving your time-saving skills, must be related to your own objectives.

But please let me make it quite clear, before we move further along together, that I will not presume to suggest to you how to *use* your saved time, or how to live your life.

Some people, like the hobo John Franklin, are perfectly content with their place in life and have absolutely no desire—at least not enough *drive*—to change it. Likely, such people constitute a considerable majority. By one definition, at least, they are perfectly successful people, as they have achieved their ambitions.

Incidentally, we've found it very interesting in our consulting work that managers' working habits are usually so ingrained that they make no attempt to change them, knowing they are wrong, even when they are being interviewed by a consultant. For example, two of the four managers in an important southeastern building were newspaper readers; they probably averaged two hours a day reading the daily at their desks, and our operations analysis of their facility didn't upset that routine in the slightest. It amused me one day as I entered Mr. W——'s office to keep an appointment, to find him reading the comics; he finished the one he was on before putting the paper down and greeting me and, on my departure, had picked the paper up and was reading it again before I was out the door!

Each of us has his own philosophy, but it is difficult to write, or say, anything serious that does not reflect one's own concept of living. So, in order for you to be able to place all that follows within the author's viewpoint, let me simply say that I subscribe completely to the great Gandhi's philosophy: since life, love and light persist in the midst of death, hate and darkness; then *God must be life, love and truth.*

THE FUNDAMENTAL INGREDIENT: DETERMINATION

The basic ingredient for success in getting things done is determination. There is no secret to it. Just that one word, *determination.* If you feel the need for success, money, position, power, fame or serving others better—if you feel one or more of these needs deeply enough, then you have conditioned yourself to take most of the steps which will be described in this book.

But the mere reading of this book proves nothing. It may be that you feel it will give you "something for nothing"—which it most assuredly won't. If you *know* that you are going to be a success (measured by any standard you desire), if you are willing to demand of yourself the learning and the practice of better methods of getting things done, then this determination is a natural (and the only possible) first step. If, on the other hand, you feel it would be nice to be able to do more by painlessly picking up some little formulas here and there, thus making your life simpler and easier, then you are willing to settle for pennies when dollars are for the taking.

Henry Ford once said that if a person thinks he *can* do a thing, he is right, but if he thinks he *cannot* do that same thing, he's still right! Undoubtedly, the greatest limitation on our ability to do things is that which we impose on ourselves by self-limitation.

I stopped in a store one day and wanted to see the manager in order to open an account. I was told he was in the back of the store. Approaching the only man in sight, I asked, "Are you the manager?"

He answered, "Who, *me?*" as if to say, "How could you confuse inferior me with the manager type?" (Of course, there is no manager type—just regular types who have decided to be managers.)

His form of answer told me he would *never* be manager of that store or any other store because he simply did not see himself as a manager. Had he answered, "No sir, not yet," then it would probably have been only a matter of time until he was managing some store or other.

The world's great things—famous as well as infamous —are done by determined design. Even accidental discoveries are usually made as the result of strenuous efforts in some other direction.

During the great 1916 offensive the Germans launched to take Paris in World War I, the French Marshal Henri Philippe Petain uttered his famous cry, "Ils ne passeront pas!"—"They shall not pass!" Mottoes can help develop determination of the type that stopped the Boche northeast of Paris.

Sometimes determination is mistaken for braggadocio. Even General Patton found it necessary to bolster *his* own determination by naming goals that forced him to use his resources to the limit. He frequently reminded himself of Stonewall Jackson's caution: "Do not take counsel of your fears."

"But after all, I'm only one person!"—how many times we hear this excuse. One person! What can one person do?

One person can compose three glorious symphonies within a total period of six weeks.

One person can design the Taj Mahal.

One person can give a speech that influences the course of human history.

One person can develop a vaccine that has saved millions of lives.

One person can file applications for over six hundred patents.

One person can rise from janitor to become Chairman of the Board of the Richfield Oil Company and one of the wealthiest men in the nation.

One person will discover a cure for cancer, invent a light-weight, high-power battery, become the fortieth President of the United States, market the greatest consumer item since cigarettes, turn a single idea into a hundred million dollars overnight.

You can only begin your personal program of time improvement with the will—the determination—to persevere.

GETTING THINGS DONE REQUIRES COURAGE

Is not *bravery* the one trait that is common to the world's great men of all time? We know that bravery is more than the willingness to risk one's physical safety in an emergency or a battle. Isn't bravery also the courage to be alone, to think alone, to act alone? Isn't it thinking freely, speaking truth, doing the right thing despite an opposed majority? Too bad no medals are struck for the rare bravery we find in business, art, religion, science, literature and government!

One hardly needs the test of combat to determine the extent of his bravery. There is an easier way: espouse some truth that puts you in an unpopular minority, especially if it threatens your income. As Elbert Hubbard said: "The man who is anybody and who does anything is surely going to be criticized, vilified, and misunderstood." Are you prepared to leave the herd?

The man who will get things done will find himself requiring the fortitude it takes to be alone more and more often—not the kind of loneliness one feels on the Sahara Desert but the kind one feels on Times Square.

BE PREPARED FOR RESISTANCE

Be prepared for resistance to your new life of increased productivity. For one thing, in one way or another, you will cause some other people to work harder. They may have been competing with you and are now merely trying to keep up. They may be concerned about their lesser showing by contrast. To some people, any change represents a threat to their security, and, naturally, you can't get many more things done without making some changes in yourself.

Expect criticism, too. People will complain that they cannot get to see you as easily as they once did, or that you don't appear to be quite as friendly as you once were or that you are upsetting them. But these are only temporary manifestations, because *you* know that you are really providing better services and organizing your work not only to save your own time but the time of your critics as well. And, certainly, the activity cannot make any *basic* change in your character.

Do not use your co-workers or even most of your superiors as models. They are part of a great majority and are much less effective than they could be, as well. Do not assume that merely because a man is in an important position, he is necessarily an important man. Admiral Halsey, during World War II, wisely said that *there are no great men,* just average men who fill big jobs. Even some of our Presidents have been rather incompetent, as have a number of "great" generals, admirals, board chairmen, religious people—as a matter of fact, "leaders" in every field.

This is by no means the time to place undue emphasis on job security. You may feel your security is threatened to a certain extent by criticisms and the resistance to the changes you are making. But in the first place, emphasis on security has been one of the most debilitating factors in our society. If you are really serious about growth, you must be *prepared* to make changes, including job changes if necessary. One healthy approach here is to assume that your organization can always replace you for less than you are being paid and that, in turn, you can always earn more somewhere else. Let it go as simply as that, work hard to improve your productivity and creativity, and you must be the winner.

Criticize your own work regularly and be on the lookout for tell-tale time-wasting methods used by others. In later chapters, we will reintroduce you to some old friends, which will provide convenient memory devices for spotting time-wasting activities.

Isn't it true that many people have problems in "succeeding" because they have too much of *themselves* on their hands? Don't they spend their time wrestling with their inner selves rather than with their real problems? Oh, if we could only identify our *real* problems and spend our time working on those! Dr. Harry Emerson Fosdick has said that the first essential for success is to *get yourself off your own hands;* only then can one be in a position to really succeed rather than to merely spend time at jealousy, recrimination, emotionalism and indulging in neuroses. Actually, work has always been recognized as having a therapeutic value. A man with personal problems may throw himself completely into his work for the solace it brings.

Mark Twain said: "Work is that which we are obliged to do, while play is made up of those things that we are not obliged to do." It does appear that work which one wants to do becomes "play" and that interruptions from such "work" become disturbances rather than holidays.

PAYING THE PRICE

We will see that we are unable to bend or stretch time (for all practical purposes and so far as we now know). We can only use what we have. No matter the course of technology, of politics or of business, the manager—the leader, the supervisor—must gain and *hold* his position on the basis of what he can accomplish each day. His work—the result of his use of time—is, and should be, examined regularly.

It is true that in past ages, and even now in some countries and among some peoples, there was and is no interest in getting more done. Again, each of us lives his own philosophy each day, and this is no place for discussion of whether or not getting things done is *right*. It is true, though, that many thinkers have written that action is to the divine as indolence is to the satanic, and it *is* true that there is a joy in work and accomplishment that can be achieved in no other way; it contributes to an inner feeling of well-being and contentment.

Is it not reasonable to suppose that the joy in accomplishment is proportionate to the magnitude of the accomplishment? Then, when you do more, you will enjoy work and life more.

Most people work rather ineffectively, using only a very small part of their abilities. It's the accepted standard. As a matter of fact, so vast a majority stay at this average that just a little extra effort often makes for outstanding performance. Sales managers tell us that it's the person who is willing to make that extra effort, to do that 10 per cent more, who makes the real success.

Now, we're not concerned with mechanical productivity—with production rates or piecework—but rather with the utilization of management and supervisory time, since it is through these means that methods and techniques are developed, and people are stimulated, to improve material production. And our national economy is quickly reaching the point where an additional 10 per cent more productivity would add fifty billion dollars per year to our economy!

Certainly, automation is not going to reduce the need for managerial effectiveness, no more than did mechanization. It will be just the opposite, no doubt. Where the cost of production becomes a less and less significant aspect of business, it naturally makes the other aspects of competition—product development, selling and advertising, engineering—more important. And these are the very realms where the tools of time conservation can be best applied.

Certain types of statistical data are best represented by the familiar bell-shaped curve. Most of us, in terms of productivity or effective utilization of time, fall comfortably in the fat center of that curve. We all have the continuous option of carrying on an average effort and remaining in the center of the curve; doing less and less, leaning on our fellow man, and sliding into the thin back end of that curve; or exerting the effort to discipline oneself to do more than the average and moving into the even thinner front end of that curve. It is sort of like a man climbing up a mound of gravel: a certain effort is required just to remain where you are. If you give up, you slide to the bottom. And if you fight, you climb to the top. I'm not going to deny that some people hang onto others and that some people climb by stepping on others, but I *am* going to insist that it isn't *necessarily* done that way.

Investors want a greater return for the use and risk of their money; we suffer from waste in government; the public is concerned about the cost of patient care in hospitals; education is becoming an enormous problem; the military burden is oppressive. Doesn't much of the answer to these and other problems lie in increased effectiveness—better time utilization—by the business executive, the city manager, the dean, the hospital administrator, the general and the admiral? And must it not also lie with the subordinates who are readying themselves for higher positions of responsibility and authority?

I further believe that honest work of any kind builds the spirit and is in the pursuit of truth. Utopia is often described as a condition of complete leisure. If leisure means the *choice of activity,* then good, but if it means inactivity, then it is a description not of heaven but of hell. Our current mania to devise jobs that require no effort and to pay people for work not done corrodes the spirit and will eventually wreck our society.

Of course, I do not recommend work to the exclusion of family, friends, religion and other responsibilities (in whatever order).

Yes, it is a little more lonesome in that leading edge of the bell-shaped curve. Rather than living half a life like many, you will feel as if you are leading two lives; there will not only be your intense activity in your vocation, but you will become more involved in cultural, social and personal activities as well. There is no need to give up vacations and holidays; rather, you will enjoy them more. You will live more by doing more. And, in the last analysis, you will have found the only way for conquering time: you will *use* it.

SUMMARY

Not everyone wants to save time

If you are ready to take the steps necessary to save time, you will find yourself in a small minority.

The fundamental ingredient—determination

Determination is the *sine qua non* of getting things done. Without it, success is not possible except by accident.

Getting things done requires courage

The doer, in his way, requires the brave heart of the hero.

Be prepared for resistance

Your accomplishments will be a threat to some, a source of work for others and misunderstood by both—and they will resist.

Paying the price

Certain sacrifices are required of the man who would do more, but they are more than compensated for by the increased joy in working and living.

3

THE BIG PRICE TAG IS ON TIME

All my possessions for a moment of time.
—QUEEN ELIZABETH I
(last words)

THE RIVER OF TIME

We spend our lives traveling down the River of Time on a ship called Earth. It is a mighty river, flowing inexorably, just as (the evidence around us says) it has been doing for billions of years. Not all of us are certain by Whom our ship was built or how it was launched; investigations in those directions are variously called religion or philosophy. There are other ships in sight, but we cannot reach them— yet. We wonder if they contain beings like ourselves. We suspect that there may be other rivers which we cannot see, flowing at the same or different rates, but there seems no way of knowing.

Controversies rage among the passengers. Much thought has been given to why this ship was built and why we were placed on it and where it is eventually going, but no answer has ever satisfied even a majority of the passengers.

But, one thing we do know—the ship keeps moving and, as far as we can tell, at a constant rate. Although to some the banks of the river seem to rush by, and to others they appear to slide by all too slowly, by measurements we have been able to determine, putting psychological effects aside, we know that the speed is the same for all.

In an attempt to measure the movement of the ship in the river, the great body of water has been given the name "Time." We have looked back and have given names to the stages of progress, both measured and imagined, of our descent, but the river ahead remains in a perpetual fog. Sometimes we think we can look into the future a day or two and even then we are often surprised. Some rare individuals have claimed to possess a supernatural ability to see through that fog . . . but we wonder.

We appear on the ship of Earth as sentient beings, as if materialized out of nothingness. Our coming is not of our choice or our understanding. And once here, we know not how long we shall remain. None of us knows how long he has to stay on this ship. A few unhappy people actually jump overboard; they commit suicide. All attempts to prolong the voyage, other than for short periods of time by medical means, have proved fruitless, even those monumental attempts of the ancient Egyptians.

We are all voyagers on the ship together. We cannot answer the questions—*who are we?, where are we going?, how do we get there?, what is the meaning of all this?* We only know we have been given existence on the ship for some indefinite period. For some, it may be a single fluttering heart beat, for others a period of many years in that parameter of duration we call "Time."

We are prisoners. We can't get off the boat and make the time stop; we can't row upstream and turn the clock back (except in memory or with things like pictures); we can't see ahead. We do have the considerable comfort that we can remember where we've been and others before us can tell us where they have been, but that is all.

The fatalist will tell you that there is a measured amount of time banked for you on which you will draw until it is exhausted, no matter what the circumstances. Others believe that the amount can be varied or adjusted by accident, divine intervention or other cause. Again, there is no agreement.

But however much time we have, however it came about, we are all faced with the same question: how do we use that time?

Analogies and examples are helpful when considering complex or obscure subjects, because they relate to familiar situations.

Let us say, then, arbitrarily, that a certain phase of your life begins with the moment you are reading these words and ends as you depart this earth (this really isn't so far-fetched; many people like to look upon their lives as beginning again with each awakening from sleep or even with each reconsideration of themselves as living beings). If you recorded this moment, then a survivor of yours could state precisely how much time remained for you from that point on. At some point in that span of life, only one-sixtieth will remain (this is obviously true, since one can divide a number into any given fractions).

When one-sixtieth of your time remains, each second will be as valuable as a minute was before and each minute as valuable as an hour. Stop now and think about that for a moment.

Somehow, through a supernatural agent, let us say that you have become aware that, of the additional life you might have expected, you now have but one-sixtieth part remaining. It is still an unknown amount, it could range from a few swings of a pendulum to a number of months, possibly even a year.

What would you do—you, to whom a minute is as a second, and an hour a minute?

Try to visualize that bizarre hypothetical situation; it is a worthwhile exercise. Whatever your decision, it would probably involve *action*—doing things that you had wanted to do before, seeing things you wanted to see before, or possibly even *being someone* you wanted to be before!

Possibly your senses would be sharpened. Where once you saw the trees, now you would see the leaves and the veins in the leaves and the very fluid flowing in those tiny vessels; where once you saw the sky, now you would see the clouds, and you would see the shapes they make and the water molecules in them and the birds flying across those clouds. You wouldn't consider for a moment wasting those remaining precious minutes and hours in many of the ways most of us spend our entire lives.

But wait—doesn't life seem to pass that quickly anyhow? Take time out now to write down the date of exactly ten years before right now, the time you are reading this book. Doesn't it seem much closer in time than *ten years* ago? Could it be that a hundred and twenty months have passed! Take time out again and watch the second hand on your wrist watch make a full circle—that minute seemed like a long time, didn't it? Yet, does it seem possible that over five *million* minutes could have passed in that ten-year period?

In a sense, doesn't that ten-year period—during which your heart beat some four hundred million times—seem but an *instant?*

And even of the time we have, which seems to pass so quickly, only a portion is productive time. We must make massive deductions for sleeping, eating, personal requirements, travel, sickness, etc. (although, as we shall discuss later, each of these activities can be made to provide some productivity as well).

We are all dying together, just as if we were standing together in front of a firing squad. The moment in time is almost the same for all of us now living, related to man's life as a whole. The future is already being transferred from our hands to our children's. Someone is already writing the obituary for our whole generation. Make your next friend, work with your next subordinate, remembering *that*, if you can.

TIME—WHAT IS IT?

The archaeologist measures time by carbon-fourteen measurements, based on the perfectly regular radioactive self-destruction of large atoms. These time periods may be in the billions of years. Cosmologists recently doubled their estimate of the age of the universe, adding several billion years overnight, so to speak. Wage rates are calculated to the nearest hundredth of an hour. A stop watch will measure to the tenth of a second. Scientists now use electronic pulsating devices to measure extremely small increments of time down to the pico-second—a one-hundred-millionth part of a second. You and I are generally content with telling time to the nearest minute or so by looking at our wrist watch, pocket watch or perhaps even Big Ben on occasion (there's even the hour-glass and the sun-dial).

People experience the passage of time in different ways. For arctic explorers, deep sea divers, endurance flyers and athletes, there often seems to be no consideration other than time. The first conquerors of Mount Everest, culminating a vast preparation, caravan and assault extending over a period of nine months, allowed themselves only fifteen minutes on the summit. The old Clipper ship sailors considered every minute golden; even after a ninety-day run, the difference of a single hour on more than one occasion determined whether the voyage would be immensely profitable or a loss.

George Burns and Jack Benny are classed as great comedians because of their *timing,* which makes of them artists rather than just funny men. Have you ever considered how important time is to many skilled professions? The sky-diver pulls the rip cord. The steel maker shatters the plug in the furnace holding back the melt. The surgeon closes the incision. The racer touches the brake. The hunter pulls the trigger. The lawyer pauses in his address to the jury. The general calls for artillery. The preacher makes his point. The flutist sounds his hemi-demi-semiquaver. The industrial engineer measures the time it takes to make a twist of the wrist. The chef removes the steak from the flames. The aerialist releases his grip on the trapeze. The news announcer watches the clock. The control officer sets in motion the countdown for the rocket launching. The entrepreneur decides to sell. The pilot calls for wheels up.

But for one as for the other—be he archaeologist, athlete, scientist, businessman—time moves on at the same inexorable, dispassionate, adamantine rate.

PSYCHOLOGICAL TIME

There are many psychological aspects of time, ranging from an exhilarating feeling of competition with some unknown, powerful force to a morbid fear of death through time's relentless onslaught.

In literature, time is considered so personal a thing

and such a formidable antagonist that it is given a personification. So often, then, do we find Time written as a proper name.

Perhaps man concerns himself unduly with the future in another life and not nearly enough with what he does in this one. Some religions consider our earthly life meaningless and devote every thought and action to what lies beyond. The society of the ancient Egyptians was based on an anticipated life in the hereafter.

The concern is not only for what happens to us after our death on earth but, apparently as well, what other people think of us and remember of us. Because of man's preposterous interest in destruction rather than creation, in killing rather than healing, everyone knows the names of Napoleon, Hannibal, Genghis Khan, Attila the Hun, but only a relatively few know Semmelweiss, Dürer, Vieuxtemps, and Schiller. Some of the most devoted adherents of various religions throughout the world are those who assume the need for destructive or punitive measures in the name of that religion, without really being aware of the fact that they are moving in a direction completely opposed to that of the religion's founder.

Another psychological effect of time is that it is considered as a personal possession; the expressions "lost time," "time saved" and "giving time" demonstrate this. The Gregorian calendar was adopted in England in the middle of the eighteenth century; it caused the day after September 3, 1752 to be September 14 rather than September 4. To the populace, the Government and the Church had stolen eleven days of their life and rioting ensued!

Scientists and doctors are busily studying the phenomena of psychological time, considering the practical application of space ship travel. (This is apart from the concept of relativistic time, which explains the more rapid "passage" of time at higher rates of speed. At speeds approaching that of light, a space traveler of the future might be gone for a year of his time, but come back to earth to meet his great-great-grandchildren!) Not only does the body seem to have some inner mechanism which keeps time—so we can wake up right before the alarm clock rings each morning, for example—but this physiological clock seems to be affected by temperature. At elevated temperatures, time passes more slowly; that is, the person's estimate of the length of a minute is shorter.

What is important to us, who want to get more done now, is to reflect on the fact that those people who dedicate their lives to the past or to the future alone seem to be unable to develop enough interest in the here-and-now to be productive.

DOLLARS AND MINUTES

Most people, business executives certainly included, have a mistaken impression of the economic value of their productive time. Their estimate is almost always *far* too low.

One reason for this is that a profit-making organization must actually make a considerable return on the efforts of each employee, whether he be a salesman, a mechanic or a vice-president. Of course, this is not to say that the worker is being exploited in this way. Making a profit on his activities, or on the activities of others which he makes possible, is the only way the organization can make a final profit and thus survive to continue providing goods and giving services to our society.

Let's take a look at the value of time. A salary of a hundred dollars per week (which is fairly near the national average) at a forty-hour week comes to just two dollars and fifty cents an hour, a deceptively low figure. Fringe benefits typically add twenty to thirty per cent to wage and salary costs, so let's compromise and add twenty-four per cent (which also helps to keep our figures simple). This brings us to three dollars and ten cents an hour.

Our man must be provided the facilities and equipment for performing his job. Let's say he works at a desk. His company, in effect, has to pay interest not only on the furniture and equipment which he uses—such as a dictating machine, calculator, intercom and the like—but also on the portion of the building which he uses, his pro rata share of corridors, rest rooms, cafeteria and costs in utilities and services (mechanical maintenance, housekeeping, insurance, for example) for maintaining that building. It would not be unusual for these operating costs and interest to be a thousand dollars annually, or about another fifty cents per hour. This brings our figure to three dollars and sixty cents.

But, we're just getting started. Mr. "X" also incurs costs to his company for people whose activities support his job—time keepers, payroll clerks, and probably a stenographic pool, too. This would add, conservatively, another fifty cents an hour, bringing us to four dollars and ten cents.

We know, of course, the forty hours per week that Mr. "X" works is only a nominal figure; the actual hours he spends at work are less than this, even after the deductions for certain fringe benefits. Time is taken for all sorts of personal reasons—going to the water fountain or the restroom, personal telephone calls and conversations and personal business. There are daydreaming, listening to jokes, waiting for a meeting to start, making ready for work, putting away work and numerous other items. Remaining conservative, let's allow fifteen per cent for these lost items, bringing our figure to four dollars and seventy cents an hour.

One of the most important factors is that our hypothetical worker does not perform his job in a vacuum—he must have supervision. Let's let our hypothetical pyramid of supervision provide one supervisor for each five subordinates. And the supervisor will earn a higher rate. The supervisor has all the same factors involved in the determination of the value of *his* time as does our Mr. "X." If our supervisor earns, let's say, forty per cent more than Mr. "X" and supervises five people, then this adds about one dollar and thirty cents to our worker's hourly cost, bringing us to six dollars per hour.

Now, that ten cents per minute is what it *costs* a company to maintain a one-hundred-dollar-per-week man on the job. But the *value* of that man must be considerably greater, since a profit must be made on his activities. There are a number of ways of calculating such a figure, but let's arbitrarily add fifty per cent.

So, where at first look it appeared that Mr. "X" could value his time at two dollars and fifty cents an hour, now it appears that the figure is probably more like four times that amount and is certainly at least nine dollars an hour, or fifteen cents per *minute*.

But wait—we're not through. Most jobs break down into two categories: the time spent on repetitive, unavoidable routine work; and the much smaller available time for creative, expressive work. In the former case, the worker is behaving as a clerk and in the latter, perhaps as a manager. In the former, he may be worth to the organization only a fraction of the amount that he is worth in the latter period. Those shorter periods, when he is free from routine chores, may be worth twenty-five cents or more every minute to his organization. The figure can go up further still if the time occurs during his most productive period of the day, such as in the morning.

It is not absurd at all to say that a man earning a hundred dollars a week spends some periods of time worth twenty-five cents a minute or more. Certainly, any time *saved* could be thrown into this most valuable category.

Apply these figures to your own earnings, pro rata to that one hundred dollars per week earned by Mr. "X." Are you a ten-thousand-dollar-a-year man? You are often working with fifty-cent minutes!

Actually, as we go up the scale, figures increase far from proportionately because not only are the support costs much higher, relatively, but also—and much more important—is the profit or gain on the time of that individual vastly higher. The twenty-thousand-dollar-per-year man, then, certainly spends minutes worth a dollar each to his company, and possibly twice that much.

One very healthy way of looking at supervisory and executive time is that each worker is, in a sense, a consultant to his company. Most companies indirectly pay out money to their own employees, in the method described above, at the same rate—or higher—than they would directly pay to an outside consultant. Companies support their own internal employees, day in and day out, at rates of one hundred and fifty, two hundred, and two hundred and fifty dollars per day, while never considering it from that standpoint. I listened in amusement one day to a group of a dozen business executives denounce a consulting rate of two hundred and fifty dollars *per diem* as being excessive, and yet every one of those men was costing his company a greater figure than that!

Where more than one person is involved, of course, the figures are multiplied accordingly. A three-man discussion at the middle management level at the two-hundred-dollar-per-week level would cost at least a hundred dollars per hour. A dozen-man executive meeting at the four-hundred-dollar-per-week level would be more like a thousand dollars per hour.

A thousand dollars an hour! Believe it, and you've moved a long way toward the conservation of time.

SUMMARY

The river of time

Time itself is an inexorable force over which we have no physical control and about which we are quite ignorant.

Time—what is it?

Each person who considers time, places it in his own personal context and experiences it in a different way.

Psychological time

Since time cannot be examined or measured directly, it is wrapped up in our personality and in our psyche.

Dollars and minutes

Few people are able to assign a period of time for an executive its true economic value. It's *always* higher than you think!

4

THE FOUR
STUMBLING BLOCKS
TO AVOID

*You cannot run away from a weakness; you must
some time fight it out or perish; and if that be so,
why not now, and where you stand?*
                    —ROBERT LOUIS STEVENSON

To gain your objective of a much more productive work
day, you are going to have to fight a battle not of your own
choosing and on the enemy's own ground. You have ar-
rayed against you an alliance of four powerful antagonists:
Indolence, Diversion, Procrastination and Impatience. If
you do not plan your strategy and tactics well, forge strong
lasting weapons, recover lost ground quickly and attack
constantly, then, very simply, they must win.

INDOLENCE

Indolence is one of man's basest traits. The indolent
mind and body atrophies and feeds on itself. Indolence
breeds war, political corruption, crime, famine, anarchy.

In business, under the constant pressure of competition, not to go forward is indeed to go backward, and at the end of indolence is the death of the business. In the human being as well, indolence is a step toward death. It calls to us like the Sirens, offering a draught of respite from toil. But the potion is drugged.

One can hardly be only indolent—the trait heaps upon itself equally bad characteristics, like rotting flesh draws flies. For one, the lazy person is *selfish;* there is so much to do, for so many reasons, yet all these things are put aside for the sake of doing as little as possible. The indolent man is *ignorant,* with all the social ills that that involves, because learning—from others and by experience—requires effort. He is often a *frightened* man, refusing to face life, avoiding it by ennui wherever possible. And laziness begets *indifference,* one of the monstrous evils of all times, especially in these times.

A creative person, a man who gets things done, finds indolence oppressive under any circumstances. For example, a vacation is not—or should not be—a periodic surrender to indolence. Rather, it should provide a change of scenery, a refreshing of the spirit, the basis for a new perspective, in addition to a rest from toil.

The Germans are noted as a vigorous people (among other things). One of their very old sayings is: "When I rest, I rust." Truly, as Richard Cumberland said, it is better to wear out than rust out!

Indolence is a constant threat to most people—those it has already conquered—but it is defeated by the will which truly abhors it.

DIVERSION

Diversion is no less an enemy than indolence when it comes to getting things done, although it is a little less insidious. It seems that the more active the mind and the more broad the fields of interest, the more diversions there are. Certainly, broad interests are desirable, but they should be entertained under conditions which will not detract from one's basic objective.

(By the way, what *is* your basic objective? Maybe you have two or three, but there can't be many, otherwise, by definition, they are no longer basic. Is there really much purpose in determining to make better use of your time if you have not determined to what end to use that saved time? More about that later.)

The ability to concentrate is a characteristic possessed by all creative and productive minds. And concentration is nothing more than the ability to ignore diversions, however enticing. (One definition of genius is the ability to concentrate—to avoid diversion—for an indefinite period of time.) The "absent-minded professor," the target of so many cartoons and jests, is really the man who has developed the unusual ability to "tune out" diversions while concentrating on some complex thought-train. To Edison in his laboratory, even sleep itself was considered a diversion and was yielded to only grudgingly, and for short periods of time at that.

Most of us, in our daily work, are in conflict with such diversions as socializing with callers, becoming overly involved in fruitless personality situations, watching other people at work, reading interesting but pointless printed material, daydreaming and of course the physical effects of heat, light, sound and motion on our senses.

I once had the fascinating experience of helping a brilliant creative artist pack his belongings for a move to another city. He interrupted the packing a hundred times, it seemed, to look at and discuss things he ran across: pictures he had painted, sketches, photographs, newspaper and magazine articles, correspondence, books, exhibition catalogs. At first, I was quite annoyed at all these distractions from the packing. But finally I realized that, to him, the packing was a distraction from creative contemplation! Somehow, we finally got through, each with his own distractions.

One of the most remarkable motion pictures ever made by Walt Disney (a remarkable man) was *The African Lion*. One sequence shows a cheetah accelerating from a walk to a sixty-mile-per-hour sprint while chasing a nimble member of the deer family. The cat is so intent on the one animal he has selected as his prey that he actually passes other deer who are frenziedly running in all directions. One of them even runs alongside the cheetah for a while, not realizing in his abject terror that his pursuer is his running companion. One swipe from the predator's paw would bring down the nearby prey, but the hunter runs on, intent on the animal directly ahead. And he catches him.

Can we learn anything from this? Perhaps so, in analogy. One must be so intent on attaining one's goal as to be able to ignore distractions but not to the extent of missing better opportunities.

PROCRASTINATION

Procrastination is a form of wishful thinking, and we all indulge in it, but it is a time-consuming activity and must be reduced to a minimum if we are to get more things done.

Actually, procrastination does not principally involve time allotment at all but merely the desire to avoid an unpleasant task altogether. By postponing a thing to some future date, we secretly hope that something will happen which will make the doing of that task unnecessary. It is true that the subconscious mind has an opportunity to work on the problem if it is not handled immediately, but this valuable tool really is not applied to most cases of procrastination because the item is not gone into deeply enough before it is postponed to obtain the proper material for the subconscious mind to work on.

We also lose time in "make-ready and put-away" when we procrastinate. We must use up valuable time in reorienting our minds to the problem at hand each time we take it up anew. Once is enough!

Before an item is put off, two searching questions should be asked about it. First, is the item of enough value to assign time to it at all? If not, throw it out. Second, will there really be time to handle it later on? If not, the item should either be thrown out or, if of sufficient importance, should be turned over to someone else for handling. If it is of enough importance that it must be handled by you, then it is possible that it should cause a change in your own work priority list, supplanting some other item.

Some people feel the best way to handle an item with which one is tempted to procrastinate is to take care of it right then and there, giving it only the amount of time which it deserves. Items which we have postponed tend to gnaw at our consciences and make our other work less effective.

IMPATIENCE

Harvey Borg, sales manager for the Childs Metal Company, is talking to his wife: "Jean, that Anderson contract was worth a pile to us—and now it's down the drain. We've got a price that's just as good as the competition, and we've got a warehouse right here in town. But quick delivery and reducing their inventory doesn't seem to mean anything to old man Anderson. I just couldn't get to him."

Harvey didn't realize it, but the sale was lost through his own impatience. After a year of trying to see Anderson, when he finally did, he became annoyed at Anderson's talking about everything but business and began to cut him off. Anderson became annoyed and dropped the idea of doing business with the uncourteous man.

So Harvey Borg expressed his impatience with discourtesy and lost the best potential customer in his city.

Victor Henderson, let's say, is research director for the Happy Foods Company. He's been working for four years on developing a capsule that, when dropped into a cup of cold water, will make coffee (with or without cream and sugar) and heat up the water at the same time. But he's finally given up, and Victor will never know how close he came to giving his company the most important food invention in years. His impatience didn't permit the proper time investment in so important a subject.

Effective communication, to a great degree, depends on how well one listens. And patience plays such an important role in listening. So many of our problems in communicating, then, are due to impatience!

Think now about some former employees or co-workers who may now be doing a good job for a competitor or may have gone into business on their own to become new competitors. How many of these people could have been saved to make a greater profit for your organization if they had been given only one additional benefit: a little more patience?

Impatience is a surrender, often, to emotion. It's just easier to let oneself become annoyed or bored than to apply a studied reason.

How many ways impatience can cause us to fall short of our goals! We make enemies, miss opportunities, lose sales, fail to understand because of impatience. As Franz Kafka said: "All human error is impatience, a premature renunciation of method."

Impatience, for many people, is a by-product of a lack of self-confidence. Under trying conditions, we can retreat behind a veil of impatience without consciously declaring ourselves inept. Where the situation is particularly trying, anger crowns our impatience to provide us a denser smoke screen to cover our headlong retreat.

Boredom is still another facet of impatience. It is always blamed on external sources—a bad speaker, a wait for the dentist with nothing but old magazines to look at, the same old people with their same old words. But boredom really comes from within and is an expression of our own limitations.

The German philosopher Friedrich Nietzsche said: "Is not life a hundred times too short for us to bore ourselves?"

Refuse to be bored. Life and nature are so complex

that the reflective, inquisitive person can find a number of things to absorb his interest even in a situation which would normally be called "boring." If necessary, you can "tune out" that which seems boring and concentrate the mind on some other subject—it is a sort of deliberate "absent-mindedness."

* * *

It's not really a question of which one of the stumbling blocks we are faced with and need to remove. Rather, we are subject to a mixture of self-imposed indolence, diversion, procrastination and impatience—at various times and in varying degrees. They tend to reinforce each other, too; a person tending toward indolence will tend to procrastinate as well.

Perhaps for you it is a matter of finding the weakest link in the chain and breaking it. If, for example, you can conquer your impatience, you will find it much easier to cope with diversion, procrastination and indolence.

Even in the best doers, we still find some aspects of the four problem traits. But with mediocre managers and executives—that is to say, *typical* managers and executives—all of the traits are in plain view.

SUMMARY

To reach our goal of more effective time utilization, we must overcome four universal barriers. They are chronic diseases of time that must be treated continually.

Indolence

Consider time not put to a useful purpose as a theft of your time on earth.

Diversion

Being busy is not enough; your time must be directed to accomplish your goals.

Procrastination

Assign logical priorities and time values and complete distasteful work early.

Impatience

A surrender to emotion brings us short of our goals; substitute understanding, perseverance, endurance.

5

LEARN
TO RECOGNIZE WAYS
PEOPLE WASTE TIME

What a folly to dread the thought of throwing
away life at once, and yet have no regard to
throwing it away by parcels and piecemeal.
                                    —JOHN HOWE

Just as there are ways to get things done, there are also
ways to assure that you will *not* get things done. So that we
can best travel the road ahead, let's first mark the "dead
ends."

We're not going to spend any time discussing some
aspects of time utilization that are interesting but do not
contribute directly to our subject. We can put aside the
effects of alcohol (known to slow the mental processes),
tobacco (on which enormous amounts of time are spent as
if in religious ceremonial), sexual abstinence (which stimu-
lates energy in other directions), climate (warmer climates
tend to depress activity), racial characteristics (which typically involve a lot of hokum) and the like. Over-indulgence
—it goes without saying—will sap your strength. Too much
exercise, sleep, drink, eating, smoking—too much anything

59

can steal time from you. But that's another story, just as is the profound effect—good or bad—a wife can have on her husband's career, productivity, viewpoint—everything.

These, then, are the techniques of wasting time. Learn to recognize and avoid them.

DO NOTHING

It is not as ridiculous as it sounds, this doing nothing. Most people spend their lives doing nothing—at least by one definition. That definition states that the mere holding of a job, and doing what is expected in a routine way, amounts to nothing, at least with respect to the development and growth of the organization. It is only a necessary function, more or less like breathing is to an animal.

Want a stimulating exercise? Write your own obituary. Right now. You might try writing it for today, as well as for some unknown day in the future. After you get through the statistics and family items, you will be faced with a basic, searching question: *What did you do?*

Did you merely hold a job? Just about everybody did that—again, it is sort of like breathing.

Even the Who's Who publications err in this direction. Position alone is enough to qualify one for a listing. But it is no secret that a good many worthwhile positions are obtained without remarkable accomplishment but rather by good fortune in being at the right place at the right time, a propitious marriage, long and faithful service, political expediency, the fact that the price was right or that no better person was available at the time. Not to say that these methods are wholly wrong. But neither do they indicate that the favored person has *done* something.

Animals and humans alike are addicted to self-delusion. If we do not like a thing—such as a difficult problem facing us—we pretend it's not there in the hope that it will go away! Undoubtedly, this is one of the causes of failure to act. And we not only fail to solve the problem in question, we also have affected our other work through imposing a burden of subconscious, or even conscious, guilt.

On the other hand, trying to do everything, trying to please everybody sometimes achieves the same results as doing nothing!

DO THE WRONG THING

How common a mistake it is to mistake *activity* for *accomplishment!* Nothing could more aptly describe the futility of action for its own sake than the creations of the French artist whose mechanized constructions whirl, clank, grind, jerk, move violently and end up as a pile of junk through self-destruction.

Some people go through such frenzied activity with the very best of intentions (that old familiar paving material). Others feel that it makes a good impression, which (they think) is the stuff of which promotions and raises are made.

To be sure, this running off in all directions may be more desirable than pure passivity, but what a pity that such a great percentage of the time is spent fruitlessly! These are the people who rush in with solutions to problems that have yet to be defined—and their solutions become problems in themselves!

Then, there are those with much less energy who work on the wrong things. They are the people who will spend a year working on a problem which has already been solved —and made publicly known—by someone else. They may be found working on the effects of problems while they should have spent the same time on the causes.

A very elaborate research effort, report and presentation with all the flip-charts, slides and demonstrations that go with it can be made—*and is being made somewhere right now*—concerning alternatives that might just as well have been solved by cutting a deck of cards or flipping a coin.

Unfortunately, there are some people who find that they can't do something big but try to make up for it by doing something little in a big way!

And, let's not confuse getting things done with cutting things close. The person who is able to be more productive is not the person who is always rushing to catch a plane or arriving late for a meeting. Quite the contrary is true: his time is well enough organized so that he is able to avoid pressures of that sort.

DO THE RIGHT THING THE WRONG WAY

The first step of the "scientific method"—that system which so many people use in their decision making without being aware of its formal name or origin—is the *identification of the problem*. Those who force themselves to take that step first often find that the problem is solved merely in the process of defining it.

All right, then, let's assume that we're working on the right problems and they have been properly defined. There are many ways in which a wrong approach may be given to the problem's solution; the chapters of this book are full of them, stated both positively and negatively. But here are a few worth considering now:

1. The attempted solution of a problem before the data is complete.

2. Failure to refer to the primary objective of the organization.

3. Working without assigning priority—other things may need attention sooner.

4. Allotting too much time, perhaps because it is an enjoyable subject.

5. Personally working at the problem when it could be "farmed out" to a subordinate.

6. Permitting emotional involvement to control the result.

The following sections of this chapter describe still other ways of trying to solve the right problem in the wrong way.

DUPLICATION

Duplication is a trap into which we might fall. Is someone else in the organization already working on the same problem? Was it solved in another branch of the organization some time before? Have research bodies—such as the government or a university—solved the problem or at least made studies that would be foolish to duplicate and which are available for the asking? Has the problem been solved in some foreign country, with the solution available for the translating? Perhaps the idea should receive a test somewhere, or is already being tested before the detailed analysis is undertaken. Many people plunge into complicated work without taking the time to search even the most basic reference materials.

Let's say that you have determined that you need to

know average human body dimensions in order to better design a new product. You could conduct an exhaustive random sampling and have thousands of people measured; it might be an interesting study that may be held within a one-hundred-thousand-dollar budget. Or, for less than a hundred dollars, you could obtain the exhaustive studies already made by such organizations as the federal government, transportation companies, military services, clothing manufacturers and various medical groups.

In order to be aware of what's been done by others, one must do a great deal of reading. One good place to start is with the publications list of the Government Printing Office. And remember the Annual Reader's Guide to Periodical Literature, indexed by subject.

There are service organizations that will keep you supplied with literature or abstracts, even on a world-wide basis, on practically any subject you can name.

EXCESSIVE DETAIL

Excessive detail, at the other end of the pole, is extremely common, particularly when dealing with figures. A good rule, generally, is that nothing should be carried further in detail than one is willing to take an item about which the least is known (remember, we're talking about economics rather than scientific investigation). As an example, look at these two methods of costing out a new product at top of page 65.

Perhaps you've seen unit costs carried out to the tenth of a cent, then a whole dollar figure added for profit! Does that type of calculation make sense?

Of course, excessive detail can be expressed in words even more easily than in numbers. It's hardly necessary to

Item	Accurate, but Excessive Detail	Reasonable Costing
Raw materials	$32.50	$32.50
Labor	12.63	12.60
Packaging	.865	.90
Overhead	5.152	5.20
Royalty	.325	.30
Wastage	.1626	.20
Label	.065	—
	$51.6996	$51.70

cite an example for that—perhaps there are some on your desk right now! (If you don't know the words *malapropism* and *sesquipedalianism,* look them up.)

Every item that comes to your attention has a value in time. You try to assess that value and give to a subject an amount of your time relative to the potential gain which it may bring. Detail, then, may be controlled by the time you assign to a problem.

If, for example, it would be helpful for you to find out how overtime has been running overall, you might request and analyze totals by department for the last month, rather than a daily report for each employee.

INCOMPLETION

Incompletion of one type is typically the result of a desire to get through with some laborious or distasteful problem so that we can go on to things that are more pleasing and comfortable. As a result, we stop prematurely. We may consider a problem solved, having evaluated some, but not all, of the alternatives.

Let's assume that J. D. Cress, administrative assistant of the Jackson Carpet Manufacturing Company, has been assigned the task of investigating the disposal of carpet scrap. Heretofore, scrap had been dumped into waste containers and hauled to the city dump. After a week of study, Cress, who was anxious to get started on planning for the new materials-handling system, delivered his report: instead of operating its own vehicle hauling small containers, the company should utilize a contract disposal service using large bulk waste units. Estimated savings: $4500 per year.

Cress's study was all right as far as it went, but he was too limited in his outlook. The hauling off of the carpet scrap is an expense, a negative approach. The positive approach is to sell the material and obtain an income. Such sale would require a study of the market or even development of a new market. His study might have proceeded along these lines:

A. Removal as an expense
   1. By the company
      a. Unit containers
      b. Bulk
   2. By a contractor
      a. Unit containers
      b. Bulk

B. Captive Use
   1. Use as boiler fuel
   2. Grinding, then use in cemented carpet backing
   3. Diversification, and use as below

C. Sale
1. (Shredded) packaging cushioning for:
   a. Electronics components
   b. Ceramics
   c. Glassware
2. (Pulverized or shredded) filler for plastic sheet manufacture
3. (Shredded) stuffer for:
   a. Furniture
   b. Toys
4. Synthetic fibers to manufacturers for reintroduction into production cycle
5. (Pulverized) to florists and horticulturists as a soil filler for aeration
6. (Pulverized) as a filler for chemical dusts, such as powdered insecticides
7. In pieces as is, for fuel
8. As is for protecting corners of furniture and appliances during shipment

Can you add other items to these lists?

Incompletion of another type results from holding on to assignments as symbols of job security. We may fear that when the assignment is over, there may be nothing else for us to do so we will be fired or that it will prove we are incompetent, with the same unhappy result.

But from a positive standpoint, of course, we should want to finish so as to add one more solid plank to the platform of success on which we intend to stand.

INACCURACY

There is no conflict whatever between getting things done and being accurate; after all, if a thing is inaccurate, it isn't really done! Nor does accuracy mean excessive detail—it means *sufficient* detail.

Accuracy is craftsmanship. Some people think the day of the craftsman is gone, and indeed it has gone for most people. But he who will get things done *will* be a craftsman!

Action taken on the basis of an inaccurate report can cause much more of a loss than no information at all. Where there is an acknowledged lack of information, at least the action taken will be conservative, and the development of the item will be watched very carefully so that the earliest possible corrective action may be taken. But where a decision is based on inaccurate data secured by a trusted person, then greater risks are taken for longer periods of time, so the cost can be much higher.

In your studies and reports, indicate your appreciation of the nature of any inaccuracies which may be built in and the range of their possible effect. The degree of accuracy you and your organization can afford, of course, will be determined by the time you should spend on the subject, which in turn is a function of its overall economic potential.

For some things, such as statistical techniques, the degree of possible error can be expressed mathematically, and this should become a part of the report. One tool that is very valuable in observing work of a complex nature is random sampling; it is often used for determining percentages of the whole time being used for such things as personal time, travel time, work time, etc. This equation tells the number of observations needed for a valid sample. Note the tolerance limit (or degree of error); most studies are made with a 5-10 per cent tolerance:

$$N = 4(1 - P) \, L^2 \, (P)$$

N = number of observations
P = approximate percentage of the total time the activity involves
L = tolerance limit (example: 5% tolerance indicates that only 5 out of 100 cases may not be valid).

SUMMARY

A man busily at work may be getting a great deal done, or he may be completely wasting his time. The difference is not apparent to a casual observer. One can be very active, yet waste time in these ways:

Do nothing constructive

Performing repetitive work may be productive but not creative; it does not develop either the individual or the organization.

Do the wrong thing

Great amounts of energy are spent on solving problems that don't need solving or that have already been solved.

Do the right thing in the wrong way

The objective may be correct, but the means to that end may be devious and wasteful.

Duplicate

Why spend a great deal of time checking something where accuracy is not important, or duplicating your own or someone else's work?

Provide excessive detail

Excessive data not only wastes time of the person preparing it but also wastes the time of the person using it.

Permit incompletion

For psychological reasons based on lack of security, many people feel uneasy about letting projects come to an end.

Allow inaccuracy

A slipshod approach to work can lead to much more dire results than merely doing nothing; it encourages mis-action rather than merely inaction.

Learn to avoid these time wasters!

6

HOW TO AVOID THINKING TRAPS

To most people nothing is more troublesome than the effort of thinking.

—JAMES BRYCE

The simplest of the brain processes—reaction to stimulus, recognition of the familiar and even the development of idle conversation—require little palpable effort. It is when we use our brain for thinking and reasoning, particularly on abstract subjects, that it becomes an effort. "Digging ditches" has long been considered the epitome of hard work, yet thinkers often turn to physical labor—yes, including digging ditches—for sheer *relief* from their mental efforts! (You may recall that Winston Churchill's release came through brick laying.)

Nothing can be more exhausting (or exhilarating) than a good long thinking session. In order to avoid such strenuous activities, we have all built up elaborate defense mechanisms. For example, ideas are often given the Procrustean bed treatment: they are lopped off or stretched to fit the preconceptions or limitations of the mind that attempts to use them.

Let's take a look at some of the ways we avoid thinking. After reading through the list, circle the items that you, yourself, use more or less regularly. Chances are, it will be about half of them. . . .

REFUSING TO RECOGNIZE THE SUBJECT

With a little practice, you can delude yourself into believing that some problems do not exist at all, thus making it possible to go on to more pleasant things. Enough repetition of this, and it won't bother your conscience at all.

Or, you can keep turning a discussion, for example, to related subjects that are easier to think about, in order to avoid the more difficult, but really important, issue. Here's an example:

> MANAGER: What do you think of the proposed warehouse in Cleveland?
> SUPERVISOR: I heard that Jerry Thomas was suggested as the manager, if it comes off. That guy is a loud-mouth.

> > (Here might ensue a discussion about Jerry Thomas, and the subject at hand might never receive the supervisor's consideration. But the manager stays on the track.)

> MANAGER: That's another subject. What about Cleveland for a warehouse?
> SUPERVISOR: I think Cleveland is a lousy city —it's cold and wet. I sure wouldn't want to live there.

> > (At this point the manager—who likes Cleveland —concludes that the supervisor isn't able to

think about the proposed warehouse and begins to question his usefulness as an assistant altogether.)

Stay on the subject!

BRANDING THE SUBJECT WITH AN UNHAPPY TITLE

Name-calling can ruin the best of ideas before they ever get a chance to get started. Negative titles bring negative responses. Would you have bought this book if it had been titled "How to Work Harder"?

"Communist" is a title that is so convenient for use by politicians; used judiciously, it can eliminate all reason in some people. Remember the McCarthy investigations?

It is impossible to be objective or creative when confronted with titles that evoke memories of failure, hate, fear or bias.

ASKING EVERYBODY'S OPINION

Naturally, there are cases where selected opinions are very helpful, but excessive opinion-taking often confuses an issue through the introduction of emotional sidelights, judgments on the basis of limited experience and the like. In many cases, the obtaining of these opinions, along with their analysis and consideration, becomes quite time-consuming in itself and out of all proportion to the value received.

If you do seek an opinion, it should be from a person whom you either feel is wholly capable of deciding the issue or who has some special experience or knowledge that will be helpful.

It's true that asking opinions of associates is a high form of flattery and promotes a team spirit, but if the people are no better qualified than you, then there should be no reason to believe that they could solve the problem better than you—you, whose problem it is.

REQUIRING APPROVAL BY EVERYONE CONCERNED

One certain way to assure the death of a thought is to require its approval or sanction by everybody. As Dr. Johnson so aptly said: "Nothing will ever be attempted if all possible objections must be first overcome."

It's true people support the things that they help create, but to get everyone involved to agree on a course of action is very difficult and when the number of people exceeds a half dozen, it becomes almost impossible.

Secure approval only from necessary people. Yes, try to get helpful contributions from other people and try to "sell" the concept to them but don't lead them to believe that the decision to proceed requires unanimous acceptance.

QUOTING THE EXPERTS

Archimedes' geocentric cosmology stifled consideration of heliocentric theories for hundreds of years—because he was the *expert*. Advanced geometry theoreticians had first to overcome a fanatical devotion to Euclid. But experts have the unsettling habit of being proved wrong or, just as frequently, of proving themselves wrong. And, what is an expert? The person whom you think is right about something. But that doesn't *make* him right!

As has so amply been demonstrated in the history of invention and discovery, a scientist may be master of *current* techniques, but he may be quite unable to fathom the future—he may even actively resist it.

It is quite true that experts can be found to support either side of almost any question. Experts can "prove" that there can never be another world war—and they can also "prove" that it will start next week.

Experts can indeed contribute to the solution of a problem, but to do so they must be involved with that particular problem. Too many people make the mistake of quoting generalizations to bear on specific problems. And, it is not really possible to condense an opinion or viewpoint into the short aphorisms of which we are so fond; we should use them only as hints and thought-stimulators.

TAKING A VOTE

The democratic approach to thinking and problem-solving not only releases you (along with everyone else) from the burden of thought but also gets you "off the hook," so neither you nor anyone else can be blamed for anything. Voting is unquestionably the best form of protecting one's self-interest in government, investment and the like, but has little place in management decision-making.

Investigate the motive of the manager who is anxious to take things to a vote. Is he trying to get fresh ideas and enlist the aid of others, or is he merely trying to avoid personal commitment through fear of being wrong? Of what value is the manager who must turn to a group of others for a decision? He might just as well be performing a clerical function.

ACCEPTING EVERYTHING AT FACE VALUE

Inquire into causes and consider the fact that there may be exaggerations because of self-interest. If someone tells you of an occurrence bearing on the problem, don't assume that the information is a clear, undistorted report. (If you do, you'll be in for many surprises.)

One of the roles of the manager is to seek and receive information. But another role, equally as important, is the evaluation of information. Because of personality and experience characteristics, no two people see things exactly the same way. "Eye-witnesses" continually provide conflicting reports in the courtroom, where their testimony is solemnly sworn. Information that comes to you is a fragment of the truth; it may be a shred or almost complete. There are two parts of everything you deal with: that which is true or known, and that which is untrue or unknown. Take enough pains to sort them out!

POSTPONING THINKING

Don't adopt Scarlett O'Hara's viewpoint and establish as your motto, "I'll think about that tomorrow," and when tomorrow comes, consider another postponement. In time perhaps the problem—along with whatever ideas you may have had about it—will be forgotten. Not gone, but forgotten. When such a backlog of postponed problems becomes too burdensome, one could begin to think of a job change.

No, make sure, when you assign a future date for working on a project, that it is really a question of relative priority, rather than mere procrastination through fear of inadequacy. If it is the latter, your best antidote is to "do it now."

RELATING EVERYTHING TO IMMEDIATE CASH

Considering cash alone would remove many of the variables associated with thinking and problem-solving and permit you to reach a quick decision. But, someone else would have to worry about the effect on your industry's over-all profitability, your hospital's patient care, your school's pedagogy, your organization's public image, your government's security.

It is indeed desirable to quantify as many factors as possible in a decision, but such things as worker morale and corporate image just don't yield easily to numerical analysis. And many organizations are more concerned with quality of service or future profits than with immediate dollars. Make sure you are tuned in on the proper objective.

AVOIDING SOLITUDE AND SILENCE

Having people all around and staying busy with exciting and interesting activities would ease the pain of thinking. But under such conditions, you would not only be less troubled with a given problem, you might forget about it altogether.

For many people, being alone at any time is a frightening experience. It is not a matter of ghosts but that they have themselves exclusively to deal with. One is never so alone as when thinking and never so incapable of thinking as when not alone. For your next difficult problem, try cutting off all communications from outside and hanging a "please do not disturb" sign on your door for an hour. You may be surprised with the results.

Many large organizations these days, such as those in the aerospace industries, have large "bullpens" crowded with a hundred or more men who are consigned to think and create. What a monumental waste, as if sheer numbers of bodies and brains could solve problems. How much more economical, and more productive, to have a fewer number of engineers and scientists in the proper environment. Such a change would also permit their better motivation through supervision, pay, equipment, reference material and the like.

MISTRUSTING YOUR OWN ABILITIES

If you assume your thinking may lead to a wrong solution, then you might as well just accept someone else's solution or merely flip a coin even on the most important matters. Some people even resort to a fatalistic attitude or reflect on the fact that it won't matter anyhow a hundred years from now.

One thing is certain: the attitude others have about your skills and capabilities will be limited by your own attitude. A sensible self-judgment of your abilities, with the emphasis on the positive, will indirectly influence the thinking of others, as well as directly control your own actions.

Your greatest limitation is the narrow scope you prepare for yourself.

PERMITTING PLENTY OF DISTRACTION

People feel they cannot be blamed for not solving a problem if they had to take care of so many immediate things that they never got around to it. They work the "putting-out-fires" routine so well that they never have time for any big problems and can pawn them off on someone else, such as an assistant. They can arrange for subordinates to keep them so buried in minutiae that they can build a good case for needing an assistant. Then, you see, they can turn over all the more difficult jobs to him. They might even have several years of respite before being replaced in their job.

MAKING A JOKE OUT OF SOMETHING SERIOUS

This is one of the commonest methods of killing a thought. Go to an art museum sometime and listen to the comments. They usually fall into three categories: people will tell you what they like; they will tell you what they do not like (neither of which has any relationship whatever to the real aesthetic value or meaning of the work); and for another large category of works, they will make up a joke. The funny stuff is reserved for those items which are quite beyond the understanding of the observer. Two people are standing in front of a painting. One grins and says, "Looks like a pile of burned match sticks, ha, ha." The other answers, picking up the humorous approach, "Why, little Billy, ha, ha, could do better than that!" The artist cannot compete with buffoons. His attempt to present a distillation on canvas of ten years of thought about the impact of the Crucifixion on modern society will have no effect on these two viewers, for they refuse to be serious.

Let's listen in on a conversation taking place in a hospital:

ADMINISTRATOR: What do you think of disposable syringes?

ASSISTANT: Maybe we ought to keep all the syringes and throw some of the patients away!

(One poor joke can be suffered gracefully by anybody. Now the boss is ready for a sensible answer.)

ADMINISTRATOR: I understand there is often an actual economic advantage in addition to the improved cross-infection control.

ASSISTANT: Reminds me of the time I was in the army; we had square needles and needles with hooks on the end. Man, it sure felt like it!

(The boss is becoming annoyed.)

ADMINISTRATOR: Have you read anything about disposables? I passed on some stuff.

ASSISTANT: I don't remember, but I did see a clever cartoon. . . .

A sense of humor is a very valuable asset, of course, but there is a time for humor just as there is a time for sobriety. A constant flow of levity is just as annoying as a perpetual grin—and far more time consuming.

What would be the next thing you would say if you were the administrator in the conversation above?

MISTREATING YOUR IDEAS

Brush them off? Laugh them off? But, ideas are the most fragile of all flowers. Although they typically grow in fertile, well-tilled soil, they can also spring up occasionally in barren ground. They must be handled carefully and nourished well to survive. Once they have bloomed, they can become very hardy, and some live forever. How many real ideas have *you* had in the last twelve months? (Most people get very, very few.) How many have you *killed?*

Recommendation: If an idea occurs, write it down immediately; list all the good things about it; leave the objections for later. Don't discuss the idea with anyone until you have considered it thoroughly and have got all the plus factors written down. To many people, an idea cast out is like an invitation to a skeet shoot, and they bang way. Protect your idea from jokes, sarcasm, experience, hunches, common sense, intuition, vote-taking and negativism. Then it has a reasonable chance of lasting out the day, at least.

RELYING ON FATE

The fatalist can justify anything on the basis that it was bound to happen. You can justify failure to pursue an idea, or to solve a problem, on the basis that it will not change the eventual outcome anyhow. It is a convenient system where all else fails.

Henley said, in his immortal "Invictus": "I am the master of my fate: I am the captain of my soul." But James Shirley wrote: "There is no armour against fate."

Your feelings about fate may have more to do with your work than you might have suspected. There is no proof in either direction, but nothing important was ever accomplished by relegating it to fate.

DEFERRING TO PAST PRACTICE

"We've always done it that way," for many is the perfect reason for avoiding change, as well as any further thought on the subject.

But in this age of change at break-neck speeds, it must be clear, to anyone who will think, that nothing remains the same for long. Anything that remains unchanged for over a few years must be considered obsolescent.

Make a list of the most inviolate ideas and systems in your organization, and you'll have before you a list of the areas of greatest potential improvement. Make a list of the things it makes people angry to talk about; these are the things that have been given little creative thought. Make still another list of the things people don't like, and they will have provided you a schedule of their weaknesses.

Don't assume that there is a good reason for something merely because it is being done by a large number of people or has been done for a long time. The Roman "games" —murders and tortures for fun—might be a case in point, from an historical standpoint. It is better to take just the opposite viewpoint: that there is a much better method of accomplishing the same result, if only you will find it.

SUBSTITUTING CONTRADICTION
FOR THINKING

Would you find an exception to one aspect of an idea and flatly contradict it? This would summarily dispose of the entire idea, along with all its potential benefits. Right now, why not look back over this list and see where you have already applied this destructive device in its consideration! For, you see, there is nothing so final as a contradiction.

Here's a case that occurred in a university:

PRESIDENT: I understand the new women's dormitory won't be finished in time for the fall term.

DEAN: Yes, we've already started turning down some applications. But we'll have plenty of room for the men—a lot left, in fact.

PRESIDENT: The dorms are in wings, with a central commons. Couldn't you put girls in one of the boys' dorm wings and have them share the commons?

DEAN: Heavens, no! Think what might happen. It won't work.

PRESIDENT: I suppose you're right.

Unfortunately, the president was scared away from further thought by the unfavorable image the dean conjured up. Yet, with proper provisions for the arrangement, many schools are achieving a higher percentage dormitory occupancy with just this system and experiencing no difficulty—in some cases, less difficulty.

Why let a contradiction be the last word if you are to give a subject the thought it deserves?

DEVELOPING A PERSONAL HOSTILITY

Some would publicly announce disfavor of a project and of anyone associated with it. They could go a step further and make a list of the things they don't like about it (but they will be performing a valuable service to their detractors, by thus providing a catalog of their blind spots and limitations). How many times has this unfortunate device been used, for example, in our own military history, with a result not in dollars of profit but in loss of human lives.

The more you involve emotion, the more you limit thought. Have you ever tried to think while you're angry? All you can do is *feel*.

Twenty centuries ago it was said that whom God would destroy, he would first make angry. Do you let emotion—whether it be in the form of anger, jealousy, prejudice or whatever—rule your work?

INVOKING INVIOLATE IDEAS

Regularly invoking inviolate ideas, such as religion, patriotism, marriage and motherhood, kills thought. Undoubtedly, they will all be non sequiturs to the subject at hand but will so cloud the issue that further discussion becomes impossible.

DEPENDING ON ARGUMENT

A good old shouting argument, the hotter the better, might just make one feel better—particularly if he is willing to take a swing at someone. Nothing relieves tension—or destroys ideas—faster.

And yet, "argument" should mean an examination of all aspects of a subject, rather than a prelude to a fist fight.

A good way to forestall an argument is to make a calm reply to the first heated remark. Here's an example of an exchange between Dave, a foreman, and June, a forelady:

> DAVE: Why the devil did you let Bill go home early? That was a crazy thing to do!
>
> JUNE: You know, Dave, I've been worrying about that. What would you have done?
>
> DAVE: (taken aback) Uh, well, I would have made sure he had a better reason than just wanting to drive his wife to town.
>
> JUNE: I'm sure you're right. But he said that his wife needs help to get to the doctor, and no one else could do it. Do you think I was too easy on him?
>
> DAVE: No, I guess not. I'd hate to see my wife go to the doctor by herself if she was sick, June.
>
> JUNE: Thanks, Dave, you've made me feel better.

June has taken a situation that could have developed into a full-blown argument and turned it in a positive direction. The next conversation, through her careful manipulation of this one, will be even more cordial.

REFUSING TO BE FIRST

True, being first might chalk up a mistake against your record. It is much easier to be a follower, and much less disconcerting. You might always be one step behind, but it's so much more comfortable that way!

And yet, being second is not anything at all like being first. Who was the second man to reach the north pole? Does anyone know the name of the second woman to swim the English Channel or the second man to fly the Atlantic solo?

There is a purity in being first; it is creative, and all that follows is imitation. Whenever anyone does anything for the first time—whether it be to provide a new business service or paint a picture—he places himself on a balance with himself on one side and all mankind on the other.

It takes a great deal of courage to be first—mainly because it's so lonesome.

USING IMITATION

After all, imitation is the sincerest form of flattery. If something worked for someone else, then why shouldn't something like it work for you? When it doesn't, one can always blame the other guy.

Imitations, though, are generally not as valuable to the buyer nor as rewarding to the seller. Nor is imitation conducive to growth.

Imitation is a pretense and with it you can pretend to be successful.

TAKING A PRO OR CON STAND EARLY

Wait for a full understanding of the nature of the problem. Don't be first to take a hard stand—that's not the important thing!

The trouble is, taking an early stand often leads one to defend an impossible position or causes one to make reversals too frequently. Neither condition is likely to create a picture of you—in your own mind or in the minds of others—as a clear thinker.

ASSUMING IT CAN'T BE DONE

This is a sure-fire way for even an intelligent person, armed with the necessary facts, to fail to draw the correct conclusions or to dissuade others.

Assume that you cannot do a thing, and you most likely will be right. But this will not prevent someone else, who has decided that it *can* be done, *from doing it.*

USING WISHFUL THINKING

Attempt to separate wishful thinking from reality. Don't assume that things will work out for the best or insist that your viewpoint is adopted as policy.

Call it destiny, call it luck. But do you honestly think either will take you from where you now stand to where you want to go?

RELYING ON AVERAGES

We are a people infatuated with the *average* (and only a little less so with the *median, norm, mode* and *typical*). Of course, it escapes us that the average is no more than a numerical representation of a mixture, and it is difficult to pin down a specific condition as being average. Can one define an average human being?

The average should be considered the *unacceptable*, rather than the desirable.

In the seminars which our firm conducts on improving productivity, we are often questioned about the amount of work which should be assigned to a person, based on averages. Of course, the question cannot be answered, but one can give a good demonstration of why it can't. An imaginary poll is taken of the audience to determine what size shoe is worn by each participant, and the assumption is made that the average shoe size for the fifty or a hundred people sitting there is an 8-B. We then ask for a show of hands for those people who would want to wear a size 8-B shoe for the remainder of the day. Sometimes one or two hands go up, and sometimes there are none. But, why don't they *all* want to wear a size 8-B shoe? After all, it is the *average,* isn't it? But, obviously, averages do not fit specific situations, and merely knowing the average shoe size doesn't help us in fitting a pair of shoes to *our* feet. An even deeper analogy can be made of the fact that some individuals wear two different shoe sizes!

We seem to be willing to abandon our love of averages and statistics only when we have to put them to work and they don't work. If you had three children aged four, eight and nine, would you buy clothing for all of them that would fit a child seven years old, since that is their average age? Yet, we use averages that way every day. It often seems the easy—and generally is the wrong—way out.

AS A LAST RESORT, ABDICATING

People abdicate every day. Some do it on a repetitive, daily basis, using a number of the techniques described above. Or, one can simply quit it all and go live on an un-inhabited island (but you'd better hurry, there aren't many left!).

Why not look at it another way—*resign* from the past, *quit* wasting time, *abdicate* from a life without accomplishment!

SUMMARY

The beginning of getting more done must be in the thought processes. But the fabric of your thinking may have many torn or thin spots which you should mend. Here are restatements, in positive terms, of desirable ways of thinking:

Recognize the subject.
Give the subject an objective title.
Seek only needed opinion.
Require approval by a limited number of people.
Give expert opinion only weighed consideration.
Avoid vote-taking as a substitute for thinking.
Look beneath the surface.

Do your thinking early.

Include immediate cash as only one aspect of a question.

Use solitude and silence to permit clear thoughts.

Trust your own abilities.

Avoid distraction.

Be serious with serious things.

Handle your ideas as the fragile things they are.

Fate is not a consideration for the thinker.

Consider past practice as something likely to be wrong.

Avoid substituting contradiction for thinking.

Avoid personal hostility.

Inviolate ideas should be invoked only for inviolate matters.

Argument for its own sake is a luxury the thinker cannot afford.

Develop the courage to be first.

Avoid imitation as an expedient.

Take a pro or con stand only after you have considered all the facts.

Assume that a new thing can be done, as a starting point for thinking.

Separate wishful thinking from reality.

Use averages very carefully.

Require yourself to think.

7

LEARN FROM TIME-WASTERS

I shall try to correct errors when shown to be errors, and I shall adopt new views so fas as they shall appear to be true views.
—ABRAHAM LINCOLN

In our consulting work, we naturally come across people of all types. There are no two people who work—that is, use their time—alike any more than there are two people who think alike. Each person will weave the many variables of work habits into a unique, complex pattern.

Yet, in some people, individual characteristics stand out. Just as some people can be said to have a "round face," even though also showing the many other factors of appearance, so can a worker display a particularly noticeable characteristic, while using a number of others at the same time.

No one has a perfectly round face, and no one uses just one work habit to the exclusion of all the rest. But these characteristics give us a "handle" or a "label" for identification.

We have never met a client, for example, who was *completely* paperwork-oriented; yet we have worked with a number who have leaned far in this direction. From these people we are able to construct a composite man who can help us evaluate a "paperwork man."

Some time-wasting traits are so common, and so religiously practiced by so many people, that it is easy to build character-types around them. Undoubtedly, you will recognize some of your friends and co-workers—if not yourself —in these personifications. As you see people at work, mentally name them, using these names or others of your own choosing, and build your own "Rogues Gallery" of object lessons.

Our imaginary friends described below have real problems in getting things done. We must be careful that their habits do not rub off on us. Our best defense is to recognize them for what they are. The faces of these old, familiar friends are all about us; we see them every day.

The next time you look in a mirror, why not try to determine how many of them are looking back at you?

WALTER WORDY

The assistant administrator of a northeastern hospital is a man I invariably think of as "Walter Wordy," despite the fact that it doesn't sound at all like his name. His forte was constructing the longest sentences ever heard in his city; they were like over-long jokes, where the punch line is a relief but not so funny.

In his book *War as I Knew It,* General George S. Patton described the North African Arab from the viewpoint of a soldier-historian. One of his observations was that the natives talked incessantly because they lacked better means of communication.

Now we have sophisticated methods of communication that should—but unfortunately do not always—reduce the verbiage (which, I'm glad to see, sounds like the word garbage").

I rarely am so uncomfortable as when I am with a "talker" (not to be confused with *conversationalist*). After all, wouldn't you feel ill at ease in the presence of a thief?

And the talker *is* a thief. He steals time. And you are even drawn into aiding and abetting his crime in an attempt to avoid hurting his feelings!

Of all the ways to waste time, excessive wordiness will fall in the first rank, probably to be challenged only by indolence and procrastination.

Some people feel the need to fill all available time with their spoken words—or written words, as the case may be—as if trying to avoid a vacuum. "Space-filling" one might call it. (If your hobby is philately, you know that space-fillers might look good but have no real value, and their presence actually detracts from stamps in good condition.)

The problem is that constant verbiage leaves little time for serious, deeper thinking. Nor does it leave time for learning. It's difficult to learn while talking. A lecturer, for example, may well be the only person who doesn't gain anything from his speech. Learning is taking in. It is like breathing—you can't inhale while you are exhaling. Neither can you take in knowledge while you are giving out words.

Not only are a talker's abilities to get things done impaired, but he has unwittingly weakened his abilities to exercise leadership. By any definition, a leader must be a good listener in order to understand the needs and viewpoints of his subordinates. (Isn't it interesting that the most exciting conversationalists are people who are really good listeners, spicing the exchange with a well-chosen comment or question here or there?) Ever try listening while talking?

Let's take a closer look at Walter Wordy.

He is probably about your age. He is often easy to spot

in a crowd because words are so important to him that he makes certain that he is heard. Then, he is generally quite repetitious. Repetition is desirable and even necessary when carefully used, such as in education, or in a propaganda device like repeating "Brutus is an honorable man." But in conversation and correspondence, it's not only a waste of time, it's also annoying because you feel that your time is being imposed upon as well. I confess that I have entered into conversations with Walter Wordy where on both his first and second restatements of the same viewpoint I have agreed entirely, but by the time the third and fourth have come around, I have developed an argument or contradiction merely for the sake of avoiding another repetition.

Typically, Walter goes into vast detail. Verbally, he'll begin driving you down Main Street and through a series of detours, you'll end up down some narrow alley with a dead end. You will not be permitted to imply any part of the conversation; he insists on verbalizing every point completely.

Fortunately, he is not usually afflicted with malapropism or sesquipedalianism. It is not normal for him to quote from the Scriptures, Shakespeare or *Alice in Wonderland*. He is little interested in sentence structure and etiology. His forte is *production*—a massive volume of words. He feels a certain inadequacy if his letters are only a single page long.

Maybe we would get more done if people like Walter Wordy were paid by the word, but in inverse proportion.

Walter identifies himself regularly with well-worn phrases. See if these sound familiar:

More or less
Until such time as
Well, all right

As the saying goes
All in all
Taking this in consideration
So to speak
If you see what I mean
My thinking is
From time to time
In the natural course of events
Something like that
Now and then
To a greater or lesser degree
In view of the fact
Shall we say
In other words
Let me say
If you will
Now and again
One and the very same
You know
Well, now
At the present moment in time
Now let's see
In my opinion
Notwithstanding the fact that
It seems to me
What I mean to say
As I just said
And on and on

Most of these phrases can be eliminated in speech or writing, or at least replaced with fewer words.

Let's ask Walter Wordy (and later, each member of our Rogues Gallery) this question: "What do you think of the Jones Merger?"

You would naturally expect this type of answer:

> Oh yes, by all means, the Jones Merger. In my considered opinion, notwithstanding the several opinions of others of my associates perhaps to the contrary, it presents a number of interesting possibilities as well as a more or less equal number of what one might consider to be drawbacks. To be sure, on reflection one finds that a good number of mergers of this or similar types are being made these days; perhaps, in the natural course of events, such an eventuality might come to be expected. At the present moment in time, our becoming interested to a greater or lesser degree in this development might well, shall we say, lead to involvement that perhaps could otherwise be avoided in more ways than one. In other words, we might say, this eventuation tends to present a somewhat lengthy series of considerations that, undoubtedly, as we shall see, should be given our attention—albeit our generally measured and weighted attention.

What did he say? Probably something like, "It's interesting, let's look into it further."

Maybe you would prefer to call him Loquacious Louie. . . .

PAUL PAPERWORK

You may have heard our times called, in all seriousness, "The age of paper." Unbelievable quantities of paper are used these days for packing, books and periodicals, personal use and business.

Paul Paperwork is partially responsible for that last category, being both a cause and effect of our current paper-work blizzard.

If some extraterrestrial creature visited one of our office buildings, someone has pointed out, he would surely think that most of the people on earth are engaged in the production and distribution of various sizes and colors of paper! He would be most surprised to learn that people are really interested in trying to curtail the quantity, rather than increase it.

Perhaps paper is too cheap. If it cost ten cents a sheet, we would all probably find ways to conduct our business without the need of so much paper and probably at a total lower cost!

Paul has that disease that seems to be pandemic to the United States: *carbonitis*. Before handling anything on paper, his first thought concerns how many carbon copies should be prepared. There may be one for the source of the information, as well as one each for himself, his secretary's tickler file, his boss and his assistant. It is entirely possible that not a single copy was required, merely a notation on his calendar. Carbonitis is a habit—no, more an addiction. The proper shock treatment for such cases is to trace the cost of all this paper work, comparing it with the value of the return. The net loss is often staggering! It wouldn't be so bad if Paul were only making work for himself, but he makes work for everyone to whom copies are sent. Carbonitis is catching, like measles, and people receiving carbons instinctively feel they should keep them and perhaps refer to them periodically for some reason.

No doubt Paul was that legendary person who told his

secretary, without thinking, that carbon copies of correspondence over five years old could be destroyed, as long
as a photocopy was made of each!

Let's take a look at a day in the life of Paul Paperwork. He begins by opening his mail. All incoming literature gets tucked away in his elaborate filing system, and a
few new file folders are made up each day because some of
the new material doesn't seem to fit comfortably in any of
the existing filing categories. He'll leaf through every magazine or brochure, marking most of the articles and many
of the advertisements for removal and filing. When it comes
to answering inner-company correspondence, he usually
adds another carbon or so to the set which he receives, just
to make sure he'll have enough to go around. For regular
mail, he always staples the envelope to the incoming letter,
in case there is some item on the postmark or return address
that may someday be of value. He's the guy that keeps the
photocopy machine humming, too.

Every few months he goes through his entire filing
system, recategorizing, throwing away a few items but
mostly deciding on what additional material he would like
to have on hand and then sending off for it. He feels that
the measure of an executive is the bulk of his files.

Of course, he keeps an exhaustive library of catalogs;
he collects them by the inch, whether or not he could ever
conceivably purchase from the supplier in question. No
attempt is made to keep the catalogs up to date—the important thing is that the shelf space remains filled (preferably with a good mixture of colors in the bindings).

If there is one strong point he has, Paul feels, it is the
development of forms. The overriding principle for him is
that the form should contain every imaginable bit of information on the subject, with room to write out the longest
item of information possible for each subject. Many of the

forms are on oversize paper, and a number run to more than one page. The selection of paper weight is extremely important, because he provides so many copies that normal handwriting pressure is not legible on the last few pages. He correctly color-codes each page, but there are so many of them that it looks like a complete spectrum—and woe to the man who sends a goldenrod copy to someone who is supposed to receive a yellow one!

Mr. Paperwork claims that he has one of the world's poorest memories and makes certain that it never gets any better by committing every conceivable item to paper—and each to a different piece of paper. They are to be found— with duplicates for the really important items—everywhere: in shirt and coat pockets, desk drawers, tickler files, inter- leaved in calendar pages, perched on the dictating machine or rolled into the typewriter, pinned on the wall, wrapped around a sandwich and so on. Indeed, it is not uncommon for him to make a short note reminding himself to make a longer note later on! Open your mouth to tell him some- thing, and his pen is poised over a piece of paper instantly.

To Paul Paperwork, there is a certain magic in those 8½ by 11, 3 by 5, 17 by 22 and various other size rectan- gles. If you ever need a special type of paper, go to him, as undoubtedly he has your company's biggest collection. He will have logarithmic grid paper, 50-column analysis paper (both green and buff), colored construction paper in various textures and thicknesses, 3-by-5 cards in all colors (ruled and unruled, side-punched and top-punched).

People like Paul can be of certain value to an organ- ization if properly directed. For example, they make good librarians or heads of filing departments, if given certain limitations under which to work. But as managers and exec- utives, they are spending a lot of time and effort that should be directed elsewhere.

Why? Because he takes paperwork as an end in itself, rather than as a tool to gain an end. He forgets that every piece of paper costs money, the least of which is for the material itself. It costs money to prepare, to handle, scan or read and rehandle, sometimes many times over.

Incidentally, a good test of the value of a form or paper is to question what is the worst thing that can happen if it didn't exist. Sometimes the answer will decree an immediate cancellation of that form. Another way to look at it is to ask what the absence of that form is likely to cost in a year. Again, this can eliminate forms altogether or cut down on the number of copies involved. One direct way to determine the value of sending copies of forms or reports is to stop sending them without announcement and then see who complains; odds are in most cases that many of the copies will never be missed and can be summarily cancelled.

Let's ask a question of Paul Paperwork: "What do you think of the Jones Merger?"

Wouldn't he answer this way?

> The Jones Company! Why, They don't have a dozen file cabinets in the whole place—how can we find out what's going on? You walk in, and the place looks sterile—nothing on the desks. It scares me. If we do get involved with them, the first thing we need to do is set up a standard forms system. Then, their order blanks only have two carbons. If we added another carbon to ours, I think we could combine it with theirs. We'll have to get some more legal size files, storage cabinets and bookcases right away.

Find the man in your outfit with the biggest stack of papers on his desk, day after day. Pay no attention to how busy he appears—just assume that he is a very poor time manager.

And start calling him Paul.

FRAN FRIENDLY

Surely there is nothing wrong with being friendly, just the opposite, of course. No one can deny that management requires the ability to verbalize, to utilize paper work, to be affable, but these and other characteristics appear as personifications in our "Rogues Gallery" because of their undue emphasis. And, we must remember that these characteristics are not *bad*. They just do not contribute toward getting things done. In certain situations, they may provide the greatest success. For example, the Fran Friendly type should make an excellent public relations man or a salesman for certain types of services.

Fran is completely gregarious and only really comfortable when in the company of other people—the more the merrier. When people come into his office, the occasion is happily considered by him to be an opportunity to socialize, rather than an interruption. At any given time during the day, you are likely to find Fran in conversation with at least one other person. It may be in his office, in someone else's office or perhaps at the water fountain. Of course, he is most frequently seen with kindred spirits—there are always some around.

In today's business world, you don't have to be lonesome unless you want to. There are the vendors who call (and you can stimulate their calling with letters and inquiries), personal calls from friends outside the organization, interdepartmental visits, contacts with both superiors and subordinates, as well as the frequent visits to the departments where one has previously worked.

Call on Mr. Friendly. You can stay as long as you like, regardless of the nature of your call. You will be given a nice seat, you will be provided all the comforts of home—you may even feel like you are in a living room. The traditional "warm-up" period can be made into a real production. Then there is the anecdote and joke phase, immediately followed by the discussion of mutual friends, cities you have both visited, restaurants you have enjoyed and so on.

When other people come to the door or walk by, they are invited in also. Before long, it looks like a canasta game without the cards.

Just as you might suspect, Fran is most at home in meetings—the more and bigger, the better. It has been aptly said that at the typical meeting, we Call to Order, View with Alarm, Point with Pride and Move to Adjourn. What are meetings called for? To decide that nothing can be done, it has been suggested! Truly, in some cases, meetings are called to tell people things they are already aware of; to enlist support that has already been given or will not be given anyhow; to get ideas on a course of action that has already not only been decided but also been instituted; to explain failures; to "discuss" accomplishments (which may have come about merely by good luck); then, almost as an afterthought, for certain beneficial functions. The meeting is the ideal medium for Fran. He speaks often and at length but doesn't venture a radical viewpoint for fear of antagonizing someone. Conservatism is his line. Anger frightens him because it threatens the loss of a friend, so he is easily won over by any emotional argument. He tends toward actions and decisions that save face, avoid embarrassment and safeguard job security.

He attends conferences, association meetings and seminars whenever possible, not for the real exchange of information they provide, but for the social contact.

For Fran, his job represents a popularity contest. The popularity he does achieve comes from his co-workers on the same level, who see no threat from him to their own advancement. The enthusiasm of his superiors, however, is more reserved because they can obtain from Fran neither the quantity nor the quality of output which they desire. He even gets saddled with numerous odd jobs which people bring to him, since he is afraid to turn any of them down for fear that it might hurt someone's feelings or cause someone to say a harsh word or two.

And about our question on the Jones Merger?

> That guy Merton Jones is one of the nicest guys you'll ever want to meet. He and I spent a couple of hours talking about the time we were both living in Dayton—I didn't even know him then. It seems that we were both good friends of the Creightons—you know, the sand people—but never met each other. If there is a merger, it'll be fine because we both seem to like the same things. Do you know, he's a coin collector, too? I want to introduce him to Lewis Breen—they'd really hit it off well. I've been thinking of a party. . . .

Francis Friendly is a wonderful human being, truly. He could well be your best friend for life. The world needs many more of his type. It is a pity more of us are not a little more like him. But, let's face it: he is not the man who will get things done.

HARRY HAPHAZARD

Howard ...., the executive vice-president of a medium-size chemical plant, was my model for Harry Haphazard. Without attempting to make any kind of project list, or set any kind of priority, he would flit from one subject to another as the thought crossed his mind or as an interruption suggested.

It is a funny thing about Harry—he thinks he is a very methodical person because he handles everything as it comes up. He even answers his mail in the order in which it is stacked on his desk. He has never understood that because things happen in a completely random fashion, the order may be completely unrelated to the needs of his organization. He thinks that the assignment of priorities, both as to the order of doing the work and the amount of time which he might spend on it, is pointless.

Since he begins work on everything as soon as it comes to his attention, it is natural that many things are interrupted with the result that only the more significant items are handled completely, and the more important items are broken up into bits and pieces and never put back together.

Because of his mania to "do it now," he just can't seem to stay on the subject. He gets confused and mixes up subjects and he wonders why he goes home with headaches!

Every telephone call is as legitimate an undertaking for Harry as preparing a report to his board of directors.

Let's see how he handles the merger question:

> The Jones deal—say! That reminds me, what have you decided to do about the returns from the Johns Manufacturing Company? They pulled

a deal just like Bee-Lyne did a few months back; that guy Trotter there was a real nut. We've still got some of that stuff. I've been talking to Miller about running a special on it, but he's been ill, you know. We use the same doctor, Doc Vale, and he says he'll be out another week or so.

We won't waste more time with Happy Haphazard— he just simply doesn't know how to organize his thoughts or activities.

CARL CAREFREE

We're going to spend even less time with Carl Care- free. Business activities, for him, are intrusions on his per- sonal activities. His telephone calls are typically to his home, to his friends, to his golf club. He is interested in longer coffee breaks and more of them, extended lunch periods and arriving late and quitting early. He has never failed to take off every minute of time due him for sick leave, vacation or any other cause. He really isn't interested in the outcome of the work he is performing, the develop- ment of his organization or even his own future. He is just a guy that does not know how to be serious. Even come- dians have to be serious about their work.

Concerning the Jones Merger, we won't even stop to quote him. His response to the inquiry was to tell a dirty joke, then leave for his afternon coffee break.

BARNUM N. BAILEY

L a d e e s a n d g e n n u l m e n ! We now come to the feature attraction, the star of our show, in person, the one and only—Barnum N. Bailey.

Barnum is the showman of the organization, although he does not realize it and will vehemently deny it. All of his activities are performed for the effect they will create rather than for a productive result. He is the man to see to arrange the Christmas party, or to care for visiting dignitaries, because with him everything is a Hollywood production.

Let's take his office, for example. The first thing we see are signs—all over his desk, table, file cabinets and window ledges—which say, "I am a busy man," and "Look how much work I've got to do." Well, they really aren't signs but symbols that serve the same purpose: stacks of papers, files, books, lists and notes. Some of these "signs" remain undisturbed for weeks or months at a time and even then are only rearranged. One of Barnum's greatest joys is to go through all these materials that are on such prominent display, reshuffling and reorganizating them and stacking them into new patterns and arrangements (he hasn't seen the complete surface of his desk for many weeks, a condition that is rather frustrating to the custodian). On the walls are various announcements, notices and lists. Every activity he has ever engaged in is documented with some sort of framed certificate, including the Fourth Annual Meeting of the Eastern Illinois Numismatic Society.

Few things are more exciting to B.N.B. than playing the role of the two-telephone man, which he does whenever he can arrange it. There he sits, talking to two different peo-

ple on two different phones. Of course, he doesn't bother
with this practice when alone—it requires an audience. He
will come to work early, leave late, skip coffee breaks and
cut short his lunch period *providing* there are important
witnesses to these acts. The palm of his right hand is
grooved to fit the handle of his bulging brief case, which is
his constant companion during his travel to and from work.
To be sure, it is a *worn* brief case. Since there is no point
in trying to impress his wife from a business standpoint, he
might take out one or two papers and look at them briefly,
or even read a magazine he has brought home, before closing that paper transporter for the evening.

There is something of the martyr in Barnum N. Bailey,
you would think, he stays late so often. His wife complains
bitterly that he is given so much work to do (and, maybe
the psychologists can explain this, she is angry with *you*
for usually being able to get home for dinner at a reasonable hour). Since such a showman must have an audience,
he naturally keeps his secretary or some subordinate late
with him.

It is hard to say why he behaves as he does. Perhaps
he has an overblown feeling of importance and wants an
audience to appreciate him. It is probably more likely that
he is so concerned about his failings, about his inadequacies,
that he doesn't want to take a step alone. He often calls
subordinates into his office when he is working on something, and they merely sit there while he thinks out loud.
The time wasted is enormous because he is not only wasting
his own time in putting on a show for other people but also
wasting their time. When the phone rings during one of
those group work sessions, everyone sits. To be sure, he
frequently complains to the caller that he is keeping people
waiting, but that is all part of the show.

Like Fran Friendly, he *loves* big conferences and meetings—after all, the audience is bigger! He is always well prepared with jokes and quips, suitable gesticulations and shoutings. It is a shame he can't sell tickets. Wasting time at meetings is a serious matter because the waste is multiplied by the number of people attending. For a meeting which involves ten people to be effective, it should accomplish at least ten times as much as the typical individual attending could accomplish in the same period of time— including the time for arranging and calling together the meeting, getting it to order and travel time. Management consultants hear the complaint, with startling regularity, that "we hold too many meetings and they last too long." We can further generalize rather safely by saying that they also accomplish too little. Most of the things that happen at meetings—like telling others what one has done, has failed to do or what he hopes will or will not happen—can be accomplished more effectively with memos, telephone calls and limited discussion.

And about that Jones Merger:

> This whole deal is going to mean a great amount of work for me—on top of all I've got to do. I'm already putting in ten or twelve hours a day. This has got to mean another assistant or two for me. I'd like to set up a series of executive conferences right away. I think we'll need everybody in on it. I'll fix up some nice flip charts and handle the whole thing, if that's okay. Will you tell the president and chairman that I'm handling it?

All the world's a stage—and our friend is right in the middle of it, taking bows. More than anything else, he is like a steam locomotive—noisy, impressive but very inefficient and obsolete.

OUR GANG

There they are, our "Rogues Gallery." The important thing to remember is that they are typical workers, *not* the exceptions! They are not failures—except to themselves and to what they might have been. They make good friends and interesting acquaintances. Some of them will even go fairly far just by influence and accident and maybe because no one better is around.

Have you seen them lately?

Walter Wordy
Paul Paperwork
Fran Friendly
Harry Haphazard
Carl Carefree
Barnum N. Bailey

There are aspects of these people in all of us, and certainly some of the characteristics are beneficial. The important thing is that they not be overdone. For example, the need for managers to "sell" themselves, their departments, and their ideas to others is undisputed—and a little Barnum N. Baileyism is helpful at times.

The most important thing you can do is to recognize these traits and others in yourself and to mentally identify them whenever you see them being used. This will provide you an armor against them.

8

USE FIVE BASIC WORK SYSTEMS

First say to yourself what you would be; and then do what you have to do.

—Epictetus

There are basic rules to getting things done just like there are rules for taking photographs. True, one can take a good picture without knowing or using all of the rules, but if a really good picture comes out it will be an accident.

In this chapter, let's list the fundamental rules of getting things done, and in the next chapter, we'll begin development beyond this point.

It is probably impossible for anyone to put all the rules to work simultaneously or even to use every one of them consistently. You will be able to accomplish a good deal more if you merely select one of these items at a time and put it to use regularly. *You* be the architect of your growth. *Make yourself work.*

110

SET GOALS FOR YOURSELF

People who have lived through some dangerous experience often go on to do something important with their lives. The experience may have left them injured physically or merely left them with a remembrance of an occasion that was threatening. Perhaps they feel that being spared has fated them for some great purpose. Lives with *purpose* are lives of *accomplishment.* That these people have achieved purpose, almost by accident as it were, doesn't matter; the important thing is that the purpose is there. Couldn't we, just as well, *appropriate* that same purpose? Why can't we, who lead ordinary lives without such traumatic experiences, achieve the same ends by *adopting* the same goals?

A life without a goal is a trip without a destination.

Let one of your goals be the building of the reputation for yourself that if you *say* something will be done, it is as good as *being* done.

If your goals are set high enough, even a failure in *complete* attainment may still provide very worth-while results.

A great leader—and doer—may combine a relentless energy with a great objective. Probably the most resourceful commander of World War II was Erwin Rommel. He was typically up at six-thirty in the morning, even after a full day of battle, on a tour of inspection involving not only his own positions but those of the enemy as well. Some of his troops began to believe he never slept at all! His victories were over larger, better-equipped forces. He once asked one of his generals his opinion of the objective of the North African offensive. The general answered, "The

Delta of the Nile." "No, you dummkopf," Rommel stormed, *"India!"*

Why do employment interviewers seem so interested in their applicants' plans? Simply because they realize that it is difficult to make a good, lasting employee of someone who is adrift.

Let's look at job interviews where the same questions were asked to two men, and see how their answers compare.

INTERVIEWER: For what job are you applying?

JOHN: Anything you've got open, I guess.

JAMES: Assistant warehouse manager.

INTERVIEWER: What are your qualifications?

JOHN: You name it, I've done it.

JAMES: (describes education and experience)

INTERVIEWER: Why do you want to work at this particular company?

JOHN: I live near here. And I hear you pay good.

JAMES: I want to be a warehouse manager. You have a dynamic company, and I think you will offer me opportunity for advancement.

INTERVIEWER: What do you want from me?

JOHN: The best job you've got.

JAMES: An opportunity to show you what I can do for you.

INTERVIEWER: What if I give you what you want?

JOHN: I'd be grateful.   JAMES: (with humor) When I get to be warehouse manager of one of your branches, we can congratulate each other on our decisions!

Actually, John and James can't really be compared —they are in two different worlds. You can readily imagine the attitude of the interviewer toward each at the conclusion of the interview.

A motto is a helpful tool in setting goals. It can remind you of past successes, as well as future goals. Borrow one from someone you admire, such as Stonewall Jackson's, "Do not take counsel of your fears," or make up your own, such as, "Never too late, never too little." In either case, it can help to keep you on the right track; let it stress your points of weakness.

Crying "Westward, ho! California or Bust!" didn't transport the pioneers West, but having a goal, and a motto to stiffen their determination to reach that goal, surely helped. Once you have set *your* goal for your working life, try to write it down in one sentence. Then develop a motto for yourself from the key words of that sentence. Family and business mottoes are more than mere ostentation; they are guides to behavior. Your motto will help to guide and sustain you.

Some people, who have success in getting a great deal done, make announcements of their goals. One may say to a friend or associate, "I'm going to take my region's sales over the million-dollar mark next month!" Another may drop a note to his boss saying that an important report will be completed within the next ten days, a full week ahead of schedule. These statements may sound like braggadocio, but they could also be a deliberate placing of pressure. Some people find they can perform better under the pressure of deadlines and observation by others, and will contrive such a situation if one does not develop otherwise. True, it takes a person who is quite confident of his abilities to use this method well—but it does work. It is an indirect, but strong, method of motivation.

Once your goals are achieved, then what? If you have gotten into habits of accomplishment, you will have no desire to come to a dead stop. Your new goals would have seemed impossible of achievement previously; now, you will work toward them with a likelihod of success.

PLAN YOUR WORK

How many of the top hundred (or thousand) people in this country have reached their positions without first planning for and then working toward those positions? I'll let you guess. And remember, inheritance or nepotism can put a man at the top, but it can't keep him there.

We do need goals for all the major time divisions: daily, weekly, monthly, yearly. Then, we need longer-range goals—a "five-year plan," for instance. All must be fitted into our final goal—our "life's ambition." But any goal is just wishful thinking unless we plan toward its accomplishment.

We must include the setting of priorities in our planning. Treat time as an investment and relate the size of your investment to the potential benefit. This setting of priorities will correctly bring you to the point where many decisions are made by the toss of a coin, while others may be given a whole year of consideration.

Don't wait to make plans. By the time Douglas Mac-Arthur had reached Australia in his escape from the Philippines in those dark, early days of World War II, he had already formulated in his mind the basic plan of defeating the Japanese and making good on his promise to return.

The great German military leader Moltke (the elder) had planned for mobilization so well that when it came, in 1870, he was able to turn calmly to reading a copy of *Lady Audley's Secret* while the actual assembly of millions of men and vast quantities of *matériel* took place. Such meticulous and complete preparation became a tradition for the German General Staff, contributed materially to the success of the various German war machines and became a model for military staff work the world over.

The history of escapes gives us valuable instruction on the surmounting of what appear to be impossible odds. Men who escape are those who plan that they *will* escape from the moment they enter the prison—as Charles DeGaulle did as he entered Freiberg prison in the Black Forest of Germany in March, 1916, during World War I. He was twenty-two years old and was wounded in the leg. As he entered the very gates of the prison, he was planning his escape, which eventually took him back to his own lines.

A generation later, in another world war, his compatriot Henri Giraud escaped from Koningstein Castle at the age of sixty-three. On April 17, 1942, he let himself down a one-hundred-and-fifty-foot cliff on a homemade rope of twine which he had taken from gift packages. He had planned his escape from the very first day of his confinement.

If you decide to take the family out to dinner, you must go through three stages of mental and physical involvement:

1. Determine the goal. You might prefer a certain Chinese restaurant.
2. Make plans to achieve that goal. You would see that you have sufficient cash on hand, the correct clothing and perhaps consider the use of a taxi to take you to the restaurant.
3. Take action. You would do the things that you had decided to do, and for which you had made preparation.

Of course, you go through these three stages of accomplishment a number of times each day without being aware of them, any more than you might be aware of the fact that, from a mathematical standpoint, every time you take a step, you are making a motion that is the sum of an infinite series of fractions. (You cover half the distance, then one-fourth, then one-eighth, etc.)

But when it comes to important things, we should remind ourselves of the three-part nature of accomplishment:

Set Goals
Make Plans
Take Action

It is not too difficult to imagine ways in which people fail because of using only one or two of these steps. One person will set admirable goals, even make some plans toward their achievement but take little or no action. Another might also begin with setting goals but go directly to the action stage without making adequate plans. Still another will make his plans and work vigorously at them without a defined goal in mind.

Sometimes the steps are overlapping, and you cannot separate them easily. The organization of this book, for example, attempts to handle the three steps in that order but sometimes mixes them up. The important thing, though, is to consider each of the three phases of utmost importance and use them all regularly.

RELATE TO YOUR BASIC OBJECTIVE

Every organization has a fundamental objective. Let's look at some simple examples:

Type of Organization	*Basic Objective*
Business	Profit
Government	Service to the citizen
School	Pedagogy
Hospital	Patient care
Hotel	Maximum paid occupancy (The source of profit)

Even the above simple examples are subject to dispute. It is possible that an organization can have more than one basic objective, but wherever possible only one should be named as the overriding objective because it is unavoidable that a choice will have to be made on occasion.

You can probably think of organizations which have the following first objectives:

Reliability
Conservation of capital
Protection of human rights
Enslavement of mankind
Improvement of the species
Protection of advantages

Complex questions are clarified by restatement in terms of a basic objective, and choices are easier to make in terms of which possibility will best satisfy that objective.

Here's an example set in a school environment. Bob Jenkins, Superintendent of Buildings and Grounds, is having a discussion with T. D. Daniel, Chairman of the Building Committee:

> JENKINS: I've made a study of flooring types for the new science building, Mr. Daniel, and it seems to be a toss-up between vinyl-asbestos tile and carpet.
>
> DANIEL: I have heard that carpet is so much less expensive to clean.
>
> JENKINS: True, but it has less than half the life of a resilient floor. The claims by the organizations representing their industries are naturally biased, so I made an economic analysis considering all factors, and it comes out about even.
>
> DANIEL: What is your recommendation?
>
> JENKINS: I tend to lean toward the vinyl-asbestos, since my people are used to taking care of it.
>
> DANIEL: Which material best serves our basic objective?
>
> JENKINS: What?
>
> DANIEL: Will either be better from the standpoint of providing conditions that will lead to better education?
>
> JENKINS: The carpet is much quieter and I guess that would make it easier for the students to hear the teachers and vice versa. Since there would be less light reflection, I

imagine it would improve vision, too. And it would surely be less fatiguing for the teachers to stand on all day!

DANIEL: Wouldn't it also tend to protect both teachers and students from slipping accidents?

JENKINS: Seems like the carpet would be best, wouldn't it?

Remind yourself of your basic objectives when you come across your next difficult choice. Chances are, it will tip the scales.

MAKE A STRONG START

There's no getting around it, you've just got to make yourself work. You've got to be your own hard taskmaster, harder on yourself than anyone else will be on you or than you will be on any subordinate. You've got one good break: you can push yourself ruthlessly, if you wish, continuously—you could never do that to another person, nor would you accept such treatment from someone else.

A good place to start is at the beginning (this is an often overlooked point, amazingly). Start right off at full power in the morning. Make getting out of bed your first positive move. You are mose effective in the morning (whether you feel like it or not), and your effectiveness decreases as you fatigue (with a little pick-up after lunch and breaks).

In a methods engineering consulting job, a typical interview with a department head might run like this:

ENGINEER: As you know, Mr. Stinson, we are

here to help you discover ways of letting your people "work smarter." What are your problems?

DEPARTMENT HEAD: I'm glad somebody has gotten around to asking me. In the first place, my budget is too tight—I just don't have enough money to operate effectively with. I can't buy what I need.

ENGINEER: What do you need, sir?

DEPARTMENT HEAD: Different things. Then, there just isn't enough space; I need a lot more.

ENGINEER: How would you suggest using the additional space, Mr. Stinson?

DEPARTMENT HEAD: Well, I need more inventory on hand. We have a hard time keeping from running out. But most of all, I need space to put more people in. That's what I need, more people.

ENGINEER: What new services would they provide?

DEPARTMENT HEAD: Why, they'd provide the same type of service as my other people give now, but we wouldn't be so pushed all the time.

ENGINEER: Mr. Stinson, what do you predict for the next few years in your department if you are unable to get any of the things you mentioned?

DEPARMENT HEAD: We'd just have one hell of a time keeping our heads above water, that's all.

The typical manager or supervisor feels that he, too,

needs more money, more space and more people. And the principal reason given—though usually not expressed as such—is to make his own work less demanding.

The man who will get things done will want to accomplish his objectives with *less* money, *less* space and *less* personnel. This cannot be done without making oneself work.

And in the last analysis, only *you* can make you work. The best way to do that is to start off each day at a run—and don't slow down. Give yourself a momentum that will last all day long—it could double your output.

There'll be plenty of time to rest in the twenty-first century and beyond.

DELEGATE TO OTHERS

The person who is trying to handle everything on his own is very strictly limiting his own abilities to grow. You must really work on things that count, turning over the other things to people whom you have trained to handle them. You want to develop your subordinate personnel, and this cannot be done without letting them handle things on their own, as well.

One principal role of the manager is getting things done through others; the only thing that compares with it in importance is deciding *what* to do. To get the greatest amount done you will want to help your subordinates in improving their own productive abilities, so they will be able to handle well the additional load you will give them.

Your range of accomplishment will be proportional to the number of people you get to help you. And they don't all necessarily have to be your direct subordinates.

It is a constructive lesson to list the various types of

things you are responsible for in a column down the left-hand side of a page, and show who actually does the work down the center. The right-hand column can then be used for redelegating your work to better advantage.

Here's an example of such a "delegation list" prepared in random arrangement by a plant manager of a building supply firm:

PLANT MANAGER'S
DELEGATION LIST

Responsibility	Now Doing It	Should Do It
Screen salesmen	Myself	Assistant
Interview salesmen	Myself	Myself
Screen correspondence	Myself	Secretary
Answer correspondence	Myself	Myself
Roughing reports	Myself	Assistant
Completing reports	Myself	Myself
Screen job applicants	Myself	Assistant
Interview job applicants	Myself	Myself
Tours of inspection	Assistant	*Assistant
Check book inventory	Assistant	Secretary
Prepare requisitions	Assistant	Secretary
Safety	Myself	*Assistant
Fire prevention	Assistant	*Assistant
Expansion planning	Myself	Myself
Methods improvement	Myself	Myself
Production control	Myself	Myself
Traffic	Assistant	Assistant
Materials handling	Myself	*Assistant

Counseling foremen	Myself	Myself
Security	Assistant	Assistant
Tours	Assistant	Secretary
Public relations	Myself	Myself
Union relations	Myself	Myself

* Myself periodically

Such a list would naturally vary with the manager's evaluation of the strong points and interests of himself and his people.

The list can be made even more valuable by indicating percentage of total time involvement for both current and proposed delegation.

Perhaps based on a lack of self-confidence, some managers are reluctant to delegate since it will tend to make themselves less indispensable. They don't want an assistant to know too much of the job, otherwise the assistant may be considered by top management for the higher position.

But you cannot be promoted until your replacement is on hand. A good test of your ability as a manager, then, is the ability of your department to function in your absence. And that, in turn, will depend on how well you've delegated.

Assign the right duties to the right people and retain only the things for yourself that no one else can do; and with it all, retain contact and control.

SUMMARY

Five basic steps are all required as part of any serious effort to get more done:

Set goals for YOURSELF

Worth-while things are achieved by people who have set those things as their objectives.

Plan your work

The decision of *what* to do must be coupled with plans for *how* to do it.

Relate to your basic objective

Decisions that relate to your prime goals will help you to avoid errors and misdirection.

Make a strong start

Only vigorous action will transform your ideas into reality; begin early and keep up the pace.

Delegate to others

Your over-all effectiveness will be limited by the number of people you will let—and motivate to—do jobs for you.

9

DEVELOP YOUR TIME

A man thinking or working is always alone, let him be where he will.

—THOREAU

LEARN TO WORK ALONE

The mind of man is a most marvelous creation; its only possible contender is the firmament of the universe itself. We wonder if they may somehow be related. . . .

The mind operates most effectively when least inhibited. There are many kinds of inhibitions. Some are imposed by the brain's complex care of the body, which, of course, goes on constantly. Other inhibitions arise from outside sources, which impinge on the brain through the several senses (no one even knows for sure how many there are).

The brain receives stimuli through these senses in enormous numbers; the subconscious system sorts out these "incoming calls" and lets a relatively few through to the conscious mind.

Stop right now and think of how many things you were aware of while you were just reading. Possibly only the sight of the printed page. If you stop to search your senses, you will be able to list dozens of things—perhaps a hundred—that you will be aware of. Your list might include the pressure of the book on your hands, the floor on your feet, the chair on the seat of your pants. You may find you have a backache or a toothache; an ear and a toe may itch; your heart is thudding and your stomach may be rumbling; you probably hear twenty kinds of sounds, from your own breathing to a forced air draft; you may feel motion or vibration; there is a taste in your mouth and a smell in your nose. But you were only aware of *reading*. You were not aware of the other things because they did not reach enough intensity to cross your conscious threshold.

If your backache became more severe, or if someone cried out, your consciousness would be invaded; you would be interrupted and would stop reading. So, you try to find or create a set of conditions for your reading which will eliminate or lessen the number and intensity of stimuli you are likely to receive—you seek a cool, quiet, comfortable room.

I remember watching a receptionist doing some reading a few years back. I was sitting in the lobby and soon became interested in what was going on. Trudy—I think that was her name—was reading *Gone With the Wind* in between her work of greeting visitors and handling the switchboard. I noticed that she was almost through and asked her what her opinion was of Scarlett as a symbol of the South. She didn't know what I was talking about. A few more questions, simpler this time, and I discovered that she did not even know what was on the dozen previous pages!

She had been looking at each word in turn, without considering its meaning. But—and this is important—she was proud of the fact that she was about to finish such a long and important book.

Reading is not the same as producing (nor inhaling like exhaling), but there are instructive similarities. Both require concentration because the mind cannot give its conscious attention to more than one related set of things at a time. Both require *continuity* since starts and stops involve time to get us back on the track; interruptions are like make-ready and put-away times to the assembly worker —they are simply nonproductive.

Wouldn't you agree, then, that we should seek solitude when *doing things,* just as when reading?

Although conversation can be stimulating and "brainstorming" can be helpful, it is still the solitary mind that is really creative and productive. This viewpoint is not contradicted by the fact that so much group research work is being done; typically, all but one of the group are merely acting as extensions of the one mind at the center—whether it be identified as such or not.

Jonas Salk had skilled and dedicated help in developing his polio vaccine, of course, but practically no one knows the names of the others involved because it was the one man—the one mind—who had the creative responsibility. The Polaroid Corporation is a big, sprawling company, but it is also one man, Edwin Land. Think of some successful organizations—in business, government, institutions, industry—do you think of groups of people? Probably not—you think of names of *individuals.*

You will be able to concentrate on productive work if you do not drain off your mind's energies in constantly dealing with others.

It is difficult enough to organize your own thoughts— but how much harder it is to organize the thoughts of others!

Creativity is required of the man in management just as it is of the artist, though not in the same way or to the same degree. What does the artist do when he wants to think and wants to express his thoughts and feelings? Does he call a conference or have a discussion with an assistant or two? Hardly. He seeks solitude, away from the influence of others. If he is lucky, he will spend a few months at a retreat such as the MacDowell Colony in Peterborough, New Hampshire, where he can even be served his meals without disturbing contact. They are left on his door sill! He will return to the crowd only when he feels the need of stimulation from without or social companionship.

Can you imagine Beethoven writing his great *Ninth Symphony* in conference? Or seeing a great (not just big) painting signed by a team of artists? No, I am not suggesting that you become an artist, but I do feel that tomorrow's managers need to be more creative in their work and have much to learn from the arts in that respect.

Let's look in on Herb Collum, the assistant plant manager of, let's say, a textile plant. He has been given the job of evaluating floor space utilization. He could approach his assignment in one of three ways:

1. Prepare a consensus of all department heads and foremen.
2. Make a personal, objective study, not involving others.
3. Combine his own private study with an evaluation of the viewpoints of others.

The first system will evoke the usual response as a solution to any problem: "Give me more space, more money, more overtime and more people." The second system will be objective but will not reflect special needs and requirements that might not otherwise come to light. Only the combined approach will provide the benefits of working alone with a full spectrum of information. And, since people support the things they help create, hostility and resistance will be minimized when it comes time to implement the recommendations based on the study. Let's hope Herb understands the distinction between working alone and working with others and is able to use both techniques effectively!

Learn to work alone! But, still keep in touch with, make friends with and learn from young people with new ideas, people in your age group who are your own sounding boards and older people with wisdom and experience.

DEVELOP PERSISTENCE

If you want a wonderful experience, an uplifting of the spirit, read the citations for our Medal of Honor winners. Putting aside the fact that some of these men may have been temporarily irrational or may have acted in a sense of rage or revenge rather than in honor and duty, nevertheless most of them were selfless men who put the safety of others before themselves. And most of them showed remarkable persistence in achieving their goals.

Key words keep cropping up in these citations: determination, resolutely, repeatedly, relentless, aggressive, tenacity.

Look at some examples of how persistence, expressed with the word *determination,* led to the award of our nation's highest honor:

> Private Thomas E. Atkins' . . . fearless determination to hold his post against the main force of repeated enemy attacks . . . were major factors in enabling his comrades to maintain their lines against a numerically superior enemy force.

Private Manuel Perez, Jr. Through his courageous determination . . . made possible the successful advance of his unit.

Sergeant Curtis F. Shoup. His . . . determination eliminated a hostile weapon which threatened to destroy his company and turned a desperate situation into victory.

Private Joe R. Hastings' . . . unrelenting determination . . . cleared the path for his company's advance.

Lieutenant Robert B Nett. Through sheer determination despite successive wounds, Lieutenant Nett provided an inspiring example for his men and was instrumental in the capture of a vital strongpoint.

Just as the face of the earth itself is transformed by repeated hydraulic, thermal and atmospheric action, so are great things achieved by ordinary men who utilize determination and persistence.

There is, of course, a considerable distinction between persistence with others and persistence with one's self. Selling, as an example, involves both (maybe that is why good salesmen are so scarce). The salesman must force himself to continue to make calls in the face of repeated refusals. And, although some men specialize in one-shot sales, most closings are made after a number of calls. The average sale is made after five, seven or even twenty calls depending on the industry and the condition of the territory.

Let's listen to two experienced salesmen talking:

JOE: Boy, I hit it good today! Sold the Clements Company another four-hundred-dollar order this morning—fourth one this year so far!

HANK: That's nothing—wait until you hear *this*. Remember the Weldon outfit?

JOE: Yeah, you've been after them a long time, haven't you?

HANK: Sure have. Look at this contact log— twenty-two calls in over two years!

JOE: Did you finally nail him?

HANK: Here's the proof. Got Mr. Weldon himself to buy one of our new combination units—eight dollars and forty cents!

JOE: You lucky bum!

Of course, there was very little luck to it, mostly persistence. And the sales manager may well be more excited about Hank's eight-dollar sale than Joe's four hundred. Although there is no substitute for total volume, Hank's accomplishment proves he can open new accounts, which is a must for real growth and much more difficult than merely holding old customers. The next sale to the Weldon company may be eight hundred dollars.

Persistence is often the single ingredient separating the successful salesman from the failure. (There is no psychological test that can measure a man's willingness to persist, to the dismay of sales managers!)

Ehrlich failed six hundred and five times before he discovered Salvarsan, which he called Number 606, a specific drug for syphilis. Edison tried *thousands* of materials for the first light bulb filament. Brahms' first symphony was written over a period of twenty years.

Persistence can nearly be equated with strength of will. It provides the means for a "weakling" to survive while the strong perish.

You can rely on persistence, a positive spirit, enthusiasm and a refusal to quit to gain remarkable objectives. On April 18, 1942, James Doolittle took off from the deck of the Aircraft Carrier "Hornet" in the lead B-25 bomber to make the first attack on the homeland of Japan. There were 467 feet of lurching runway in front of his plane, but he took off with 100 feet to spare. It had been clearly established by experts before that time that the "minimum" runway required for a B-25 take-off was 700 feet!

One definition of defeat is the mere admission of defeat. A battle is lost by the leader who has decided that he will not win. A glorious example of this viewpoint is the fight between *Bonhomme Richard,* captained by John Paul Jones, against the British *Serapis* during the War of 1812. The American ship was almost completely destroyed and in a sinking condition, with most of the crew and guns out of commission. Jones won that battle by refusing to concede a defeat that was apparent to everyone but himself.

Progress is a tug of war, with Resistance to change on one side and Persistence for change on the other. Are you ready to choose sides?

EMBRACE CHANGE

Physiologists tell us that the body is in a continuous state of change. So many thousands of cells are undergoing change at any one time that the body is scarcely the same organism from one hour to the next. It is unfortunate that in such a constantly changing body is housed a brain that, mentally, is so resistant to change!

Resistance to change, which seems to be a "natural" human reaction, is based on fear. We find it easier to live with the status quo, even if it is an unhappy condition; we do not know what effects change will bring, either as a bad result or in just getting through it.

"Don't rock the boat" is often the byword. But how can anything be improved without change? Change is a

requirement of the universe—nothing ever stays the same—
yet we resist it.

If you are to advance, you must not merely tolerate
change—you must *embrace* it. You must get in the habit
of making changes. You can warm up to it by forcing a
change in some small things: change your bedtime, shoe
style, newspaper, brand of toothpaste. Learn to know
change by conditioning yourself to it.

Naturally, there is no point in change for its own sake
—even vandalism would fall in that category. Actually, the
most natural change is a wearing away, a running down.
But the balance is too finely poised to hold a midpoint. We
must determine the *direction* of change.

Look around you, right now. If you expect to see the
same things five years from now, you are mistaken. Even if
the *things* are the same, your way of using them will be
different. But even more important, *you* will be different,
by design or not.

You *will* change; your only choice is partially directing the course of the change.

There is no abdication from change—except in death.

SEEK THE REAL TRUTH

Anything can be justified or rationalized.
Anything.
Anything. The murder of gypsies and Jews by the
Nazis, persecution of Negroes by other Americans, civil dis-
obedience, stealing from the government, infidelity, injus-
tice, war—they can all be made to appear quite legal, even
holy. If one responds with emotion rather than reason, with
prejudice rather than understanding, then anything can be
satisfactorily "explained away." And, playing a significant

role in this difficulty in human affairs is the concept of "conjugate principles" which states that either side of a question can be fully justified, though from a different standpoint. The classic example, often cited, is the American Revolution. The British Government was obliged to protect its sovereignty over one of its colonies, while the Americans felt obliged to protect their individual rights.

The weight of public opinion, the preponderance of literature or the duration of a concept, as history has proven many, many times, may have nothing to do with actual value or truth. A geocentric cosmology—the earth as the center of the universe—was a "fact" for almost all of human history and believed by just about every person alive until the days of Copernicus. His heliocentric cosmology—the sun as the center of the universe—was developed in opposition to the Church (because of its religious aspect, in removing man from the center of all activity), the state (in support of the Church) and almost the entire thinking public (because of the Church and state viewpoint). And now, even that theory has been discarded in favor of a cosmos which has expanded (and perhaps contracted and expanded again) from some undefined point.

One must learn to think beyond the environmental context. Citizens of the U.S.S.R. are daily assailed with literature, conversation and official policy that "proves" our democracy to be a degenerate system that does not truly serve the people. This, then, has become the viewpoint of some two hundred million Russians, but it hardly makes it correct.

If you accept everything at face value, you will miss a great deal and will be led to make a number of incorrect decisions. Here are some "facts" that might come to your desk, compared with the real truth which might be discovered by another, or deeper, inquiry:

Report from a foreman: Jackson and Danko just can't get along—one of them will have to go. *The real truth:* Jackson and Danko enjoy ribbing each other but really are friends. Their production is above average. Their banter, however, gets on the foreman's nerves. *Action:* Straighten out the foreman, or transfer him to another crew.

Complaint from Percy Seale: You have given me too much to do—I just can't get it all done in a day. *The real truth:* Percy has been assigned a reasonable day's work but has been given more to do than Bob Dulaney, who does a similar job nearby. *Action:* Balancing the work loads by giving Dulaney more to do would remove the discontent and also get more done.

Report from an assistant: The workers have a list of nine complaints. *The real truth:* The nine complaints are of no consequence. The workers have only one serious complaint—they want better supervision. The other items are merely a reflection of this discontent which the workers are unable to verbalize. *Action:* Instigate a supervisory training program, with emphasis on motivation, human relations and knowledgeability.

Inter-office memo from the comptroller: Both overtime and number of employees are excessive in the plant housekeeping function; eliminate the overtime, cut the staff, or both. *The real truth:* To meet the deadline on the rush job, production foremen have impressed custodians into part-time materials handling; they are only spending about half of their time in cleaning. *Action:* First, see that the production departments are charged for the time. Then, consider centralizing custodial

supervision to prevent their use for other purposes, to avoid accidents, pay-rate problems and
discontent.

We have serious problems in communication, because
what is *said* is often different from what is *meant;* what is
said may even be different from what is *heard.*

Dr. Jesse S. Nirenberg, in his book *Getting Through
to People* (Prentice-Hall, 1963), tells us that we must do
more than exchange words in order to have effective communication; we must have a meeting of the minds through
a use of human forces. We must overcome the tendency of
people to think their own thoughts rather than to listen, to
let their attention wander, to hear only that which they
want to hear, to make unwarranted assumptions. We must
deal with the emotional needs of the people involved to
determine the *real* meaning; we must look below the surface.

Will anything less than the truth satisfy *you?*

DEVELOP A QUESTIONING ATTITUDE

Just how insistent a questioning attitude have you?
Are you willing to ride in an automobile, use a television
set, even write with a ball-point pen without knowing how
they work? Do you talk about your automobile's *differen-
tial* and *carburetor* without really knowing how they
function?

Look beyond the obvious—it is a matter of sharpen-
ing the perception. Most people take advertising, for example, at face value; yet a great deal of it is absolutely meaningless. One of the most hilarious comedies on the American
scene is to witness how each of a dozen different cigarette
brands incontrovertibly proves it is the best brand of all—

and by how far! A handkerchief in a dress suit pocket could really be nothing more than a piece of cardboard, on which is printed an advertisement for the cleaner, with a little bit of cloth sewn on top; what looks like a severe wound may be a piece of painted plaster wrapped around an uninjured person's limb to simulate a wound for first aid teaching purposes.

When reading, will you go right through a word without stopping to learn what it means? If so, perhaps part of the trouble is not having a dictionary conveniently at hand. Most people need *four* dictionaries, one each for the living room (or library or den), office, bedroom and bathroom (that's right). Finally, if one travels a good deal, a pocket dictionary in the briefcase is also helpful.

Many people repeatedly use words in their daily conversation without knowing what they mean. We all know that Little Miss Muffet sat on her tuffet eating her curds and whey, but what is a *tuffet* and what are *curds* and *whey?* How many times have you seen a sign that read *grist mill;* yet, what is *grist?* What did you do when you *plighted* your *troth?* What is a *denizen* of the deep? A *pied* piper?

How does an opera differ from an operetta? A meteor from a meteorite? Etching from engraving? Iraq from Iran? Schist from schism? Flammable from inflammable?

Make a list of words and things that you do not understand. Cross them off when you have learned them. If you are building yourself a road to the future, you had better fill in some of the holes!

SUMMARY

Learn to work alone

Creative effectiveness is diluted by numbers.

Develop persistence

Big doors are not easily opened.

Embrace change

There *will* be change, but you may either be the changer or the changed.

Seek the real truth

Effective action must involve more than face values.

Develop a questioning attitude

The man who *does* is the man who *wonders*.

10

USE POSITIVE WORK
TECHNIQUES

*There's only one corner of the universe you can
be certain of improving, and that's your own self.*
—ALDOUS HUXLEY

Make the time you have more valuable by using the productive systems in this chapter.

TAKE A FRESH APPROACH

Get in the habit of considering a subject from more than one viewpoint. The same approach to every problem —typically a head-on, matter-of-fact approach—provides only a narrow latitude of understanding. Broaden your scope with other techniques:

Reductio ad absurdum

Reduction to the absurd—the carrying of a trend or proposal to a ridiculous extreme—can expose a fatal weakness or support a sound viewpoint. Here's

139

an example of how this method can help solve problems:

AUTO MANUFACTURER: Have you come up with the lighting arrangement for the new models?

DESIGNER: The trend seems to be toward more lamps. The public likes it. We're considering four front and four rear lights.

AUTO MANUFACTURER: How far have you gone in your considerations?

DESIGNER: Well, two each is the absolute minimum, and over four would be too expensive.

AUTO MANUFACTURER: Let's reduce this thing to the absurd and see where it gets us. The lowest number is one. What if we had *one* lamp?

DESIGNER: (after consideration) For one lamp to serve both front and rear lighting, it would have to be on top—or underneath—the car.

AUTO MANUFACTURER: Could it work?

DESIGNER: Yes, if the pattern and intensity of the beams could change—yes, that could even be done automatically. And it could also be used as a distress signal.

AUTO MANUFACTURER: What about having *no* lamps?

DESIGNER: We'd have to have something to take their place—a luminous patch or something. Or maybe something like radar that can be received as light.

AUTO MANUFACTURER: What about a million lamps?

DESIGNER: That would be so many they would be in a solid mass or a strip all around the car. The equivalent would be a band of light all around, maybe red in the back, yellow on the side and white in front.

AUTO MANUFACTURER: Bring me some designs and costs.

DESIGNER: We'd have to have some new inventions to do some of these things:

AUTO MANUFACTURER: Coordinate with our Chief of Research—he'll give you what you want.

DESIGNER: We won't be able to meet the deadline.

AUTO MANUFACTURER: Do it along with your current study, and we'll be covered.

Assumption of Accomplishment

Assume that what you're considering is *already* the case. What is its effect? What would be the desirability, then, of changing to what you are actually now experiencing? Example:

PLANT ENGINEER: What we need is a box-making machine.

PLANT MANAGER: I've heard you say that a number of times, Gene. Now, let's assume that your machine were sitting out there in the receiving area, paid for and consigned to you. What would you do with it?

PLANT ENGINEER: What?

PLANT MANAGER: Think about it.

PLANT ENGINEER: Let's see. . . . Well, first, we'd have to prepare an area for its operation. That would mean room for the machine—it's pretty big—working room, storage of the roll stock and work in progress. Finished storage would be about the same as now, maybe a little less.

PLANT MANAGER: Where would it go?

PLANT ENGINEER: Well, we really don't have room now. But we would if we built the new addition we've been talking about.

PLANT MANAGER: Then it would be ready to go?

PLANT ENGINEER: Well, you'd have to hire a couple of men to run it and train them as well. I guess the manufacturer would help us with that. And then there's utilities, too. And waste disposal. And fire protection. And safety guards. And. . . .

PLANT MANAGER: Gene, do you think, subconsciously, you may be pushing this to justify the possible new construction?

PLANT ENGINEER: Well, Dwain, I never thought of that, but now, I wouldn't doubt it!

Distortion of Time

Consider that the time involved in the consideration of a problem is considerably shortened or lengthened. If that changes things favorably, then perhaps a way can be found to create the same results in actuality.

If, for instance, someone feels that the sales management set-up would be greatly improved in five years, find out what is expected to happen over that period of time and, if favorable, consider making it happen *now*. In this case, perhaps a retirement was involved, and the man concerned can be shifted to another position more favorable to the company's growth.

Assumption of Error

Pretend that each of the "facts" involved, in turn, is in error. How does this affect the outcome? What then can be done to strengthen or change those "facts"? Here's a sample case in point:

BUILDING MANAGER: I see that the Central Building has put in automatic elevators. I think we should consider it again.

SUPERINTENDENT: Like I told you before, the union would strike, and where would we be?

BUILDING MANAGER: We'd be struck. What would happen if they didn't strike, though?

SUPERINTENDENT: Why, it would be great. We'd be able to give our tenants better service and save a great deal of money besides, you know that.

BUILDING MANAGER: Yes I know that, but I'm not as sure as you are that we'll be struck. Why do you think so?

SUPERINTENDENT: It's a fact, I tell you. Some of the fellows actually told me they would.

BUILDING MANAGER: I think we've been running scared. In the first place, it's *our* decision to make. Furthermore, Central wasn't struck.

SUPERINTENDENT: But they've got a different union.

BUILDING MANAGER: But it is a union, and they didn't strike. I suggest we discuss this with the union. I think they will listen to reason. Unless we put in automatics, we are going to lose more and more tenants through excessive rates and poor elevator service —not to mention the appearance of the elevators themselves. This would have to mean a cutting of the staff just to stay in business. And we can guarantee that we will make the change through normal attrition, with no one being laid off.

SUPERINTENDENT: It is true that public opinion is on our side.

BUILDING MANAGER: Yes, and right is on our side, too. We will get our new elevators without a strike, and our employees will be working for a company with a brighter future.

Assume Another Role

What would you do if you were your most successful competitor, your enemy, on the verge of bankruptcy, enjoying great prosperity or any of a number of things you may not really be? If it would change your actions or policies, why not consider changing them without waiting for the other events to occur and evaluate the effect it would have.

Suppose, then, that your company were breaking even instead of making reasonable profits. What would you be doing that would differ from current practice? Would you—

- Curtail advertising
- Increase advertising
- Eliminate fringe departments
- Reduce research
- Increase research
- Close some branches
- Change prices
- Change commissions
- Change the product line
- Reduce indirect labor
- Curtail capital investment
- Increase contract services
- Increase subcontracts
- Consider mergers
- Consider acquisitions

- Verticalize production
- Diversify
- Eliminate paperwork
- Change the committee structure
- Re-evaluate fringe benefits
- Import management talent
- Lower the permissible retirement age.
- Lower the mandatory retirement age
- Change discount terms
- Require all travel by tourist class
- Tighten stock shrinkage security
- Enforce break and lunch hours
- Eliminate loss or break-even services
- Re-evaluate old cost-improvement ideas
- Control utilities usage
- Establish secretarial pools
- Change accounting methods

If so, why not consider doing some of those things *now?*

Identify with an Historical Figure

A perfect moral viewpoint, for example, is the too-rarely used "What would Christ have done?" Or, from other viewpoints, what would have been Napoleon's course of action? What would P. T. Barnum do? Edison? Shakespeare? Gandhi? Churchill? Da Vinci? Take the time to select your favorite person in history, the one *you* would most want to be like. (It's a little risky to use a contemporary as a model, but it still works.) Then, regularly use *his* frame of reference as a thought test to help you make decisions.

Mentally Start Over

Problems are typically solved by improving one aspect of an existing arrangement. In many cases, though, problems can be solved quicker and more completely without reference to existing solutions; we merely take a creative approach to securing the desired objective. Mentally, one pretends that the job or service had never been done before. Now, what's the best way of doing it? Example:

SALES MANAGER: We've got to give our men better service; we can't meet the local competition otherwise. We need more warehouses, and we need to stock all our warehouses better.

PRESIDENT: George, the nature of our business has seemed to change; we have so many items now that need modification before shipment. How should we handle that?

SALES MANAGER: We'll have to have a mechanic and maybe an engineer at each warehouse, with a good supply of parts.

PRESIDENT: But it's impossible to have all the parts even in the biggest warehouse. And in this business, it takes a lot of time and money to train engineers and mechanics. Yet, they would only stay busy a small amount of the time in a warehouse.

SALES MANAGER: We've got to do *something*. Larry. Things are getting serious.

PRESIDENT: George, suppose you were going into business tomorrow in this line and had plenty of capital, good products, a top sales force and your customers all lined up. How would you handle distribution?

SALES MANAGER: (after a pause for deliberation) I think I'd locate a combination plant and distribution center in the east and another in the west—maybe Philadelphia and San Francisco. We'd have a top team of engineers and mechanics at both places—I'd operate them independently, with their own budgets. Then, set up a complete communications network—teletype, telephone, what have you. Salesmen and customers could call in orders, and they would be shipped out by air freight.

PRESIDENT: What about warehouses?

SALES MANAGER: Wouldn't need any. Although our stuff is heavy, air freight rates have gone down. We would need regional offices and display rooms, all right, but we could save hundreds of thousands in warehouse rental, personnel and inventory. We might even want to have a plane or two of our own at each of the two plants for "special delivery."

PRESIDENT: I've been thinking along these lines too, George. You've given me some real good ideas, and I'm glad we agree that we should move in this direction.

DO IT WELL

A few years ago, while on business in Chicago, I enjoyed an experience I'll never forget. Three members of our firm and I had just finished dinner at a famous old restaurant when a busboy walked up and began to clear the table.

We began to notice his work, and our idle conversation fell off while we watched him with rapt attention. He had begun by placing one of the dinner plates in the palm of his left hand and continued by arranging the other large plates on top of it in a rosette pattern, diminishing to smaller plates and other crockery until there was quite a stack piled up on his left hand and forearm. On top of all this, he placed the glasses, silverware and other pieces; then, with his right hand, he cleaned the table thoroughly, replacing the salt and pepper containers carefully in the middle of the table—and finally asked if there was any service he could provide us at that point! We shook our heads and watched him walk away, with perhaps fifty pieces of dinnerware carried on his left arm and a neatly folded towel on the other.

We looked at each other. We had spent the whole day in a seminar talking about productivity. "Praise be," someone said, "we've finally seen a craftsman in Chicago!"

With the advent of mass production and planned obsolescence, it has been said that the day of the craftsman is over. This may be true with respect to the actual production of consumer goods, but it can never be true for leaders and executives who want to get things done. If things are not done well, then they are simply not done at all; since the desired result may not be achieved, there may be a hidden failing or the whole thing may backfire.

Just as getting things done doesn't mean always being late or rushing to catch a train, neither does it mean rushing through important work that needs careful attention. And if it isn't important work, then someone else should be doing it.

MAKE USE OF YOUR SPARE TIME

There really is no such thing as spare time.

Time is time, and the labels we give to increments of of it are for convenience only. For most people "spare time" probably means time the use of which has not been determined by others. There seems to be such a small amount of time available to us that we can "call our own," that spare time becomes a precious commodity indeed!

The world would be a different place if some people had failed to use their "spare time" productively. We would not have many of the inventions of Edison, the creations of Michelangelo, the philosophy of Spinoza. A serious research of the fruits of "spare time" would undoubtedly result in an impressive catalog of ideas, inventions, creations and accomplishments—benefits we would not otherwise enjoy. Many ideas (not all good) have even come to us from men in prison—Hitler, Gandhi, the Bird Man of Alcatraz. Most books, other than by professional novelists, are written in "spare time."

As the national average work week goes down—for everybody except executives and the self-employed—there will be a vast quantity of spare time made available. Most of it will be spent in amusement and other forms of self-gratification, but the upsurge in adult education gives us hope that a reasonable proportion of that time will also be spent in learning and applying new knowledge to the solution of more problems.

How do you spend your time when traveling, waiting in terminals, sitting in waiting rooms when seeking an audience, eating alone? Why not in reading?

USE YOUR SUBCON-
SCIOUS MIND

Have you ever awakened in the morning, or even in the middle of the night, with a good idea or with a solution to a problem that has been bothering you? Probably so; it was the result of your subconscious mind working on information which you had previously fed into the conscious mind.

For the subconscious thought to be of any value to you, it must be re-transferred to the conscious mind, and this is most likely to take place just as one is waking (or under the influence of certain drugs). For this reason, the image is a fleeting one and may escape altogether unless it is written down immediately. Many people use the good habit of keeping pencil and paper handy on the night table and writing down anything which occurs to them immediately on waking.

All subconscious activity isn't accidental, and you don't have to wait for something to happen. You can actually "stoke" the subconscious by reviewing factual information relating to a given problem before retiring and "telling" the subconscious to get to work! It works often enough to be a very helpful method of getting things done. It does take a little practice and getting used to, and please don't substitute insomnia for it!

The day will surely come when a machine will be able

to feed great masses of factual information into our memories while the conscious mind is asleep; this would save a great deal of time spent in reading and stimulate many more subconscious ideas. And drugs will help us release stored information. Until that time comes, though, let's use what we have.

General George S. Patton, of Third Army fame, often came up with brilliant tactical and strategic plans during World War II. Most of these plans, with all their details complete, just "popped into his head," as he described it to friends.

But he realized that such ideas were the result of lengthy subconscious "cooking," and he had prepared well for this by the accumulation of a great mass of pertinent data and experience. Even when he and Mrs. Patton took their vacations, he would go to a country with a rich military history and spend his time in a region which appeared to have future military significance. When he moved his army through the bocage regions of France in 1944, he carried with him the same type of ordinary road map he used when visiting that area two decades before; all the other data was in his mind.

The problems that confronted him, then, were bathed in a nutrient broth, in a mind crowned with years of intensive study and contemplation of every conceivable aspect of military history, tested by as much experience as he could get. No wonder he would wake up at three in the morning with a new plan to breach the West Wall!

USE METHODS ENGIN-
EERING PRINCIPLES

The byword of the *industrial engineer* is: "With sufficient study, any method can be improved." This applies not
only to factory environment but also to any situation where
work is performed. H. B. Maynard defines industrial engineering as: "The engineering approach applied to all factors, including the human factor, involved in the production
and distribution of products or services."

The foundations of industrial engineering and methods
improvement were laid by Frederick W. Taylor, Lawrence
L. Gantt, Frank and Lillian Gilbreth and others around the
turn of the century. One of the earliest publications of real
value was Taylor's *Shop Management,* printed in 1903,
which developed a good deal of interest in time study. Independently, Gilbreth was conducting his experiments in motion study while Gantt was calling attention to the importance of leadership and of considering the human factor.
The earliest term used for the concept was *scientific management,* but this met with a violent reaction. The AF of L
described the "Taylor system" in one of its resolutions as "a
diabolical scheme for the reduction of the human being to
the condition of a mere machine."

Now, the more up-to-date and precise titles *management consulting* and *methods engineering* are tending to replace *industrial engineering* in some fields.

There is a feeling among methods engineers that there
is "one best way" of performing any given job. They have
a number of practical techniques that can be of value to
you. For example, Dr. Gerald Nadler in his *Work Design*
(Richard D. Irwin, Inc., 1963) has codified and detailed

the creative, rather than corrective, approach to problem-solving by the methods engineer.

Why not learn more about them?

REMEMBER THE HUMAN ELEMENT

You are a sales manager, let's say, and you are losing some of your best salesmen. You questioned them during an exit interview, and everything seemed all right—but why did they *really* leave? They admitted that their contracts were handled scrupulously correctly, that they were treated fairly, that there was nothing illegal in the accounting for their commissions or in charges against their accounts. But, men who were earning over twenty thousand dollars per year were leaving "for better opportunity," yet taking jobs that earned less in just the same type of business.

But, what the salesmen didn't say, and perhaps did not even realize as being the cause of their termination, was that they were being plagued with account charges that rankled them. Here they were, making thousands of dollars of profit for their company, yet receiving charges for forty-cent telephone calls or twenty cents worth of postage. One of the men who left was particularly disgruntled about three errors in his commission statement, all in favor of the company. Another didn't like the way he was treated on the telephone when he called in five rush orders in one week's time.

A decision, a way of doing business, may be perfectly legal, fair, just and business-like, but if it doesn't take into account human emotions, then it may be wrong, completely wrong. In this case, no one had ever questioned the salesmen to determine their attitude about the way they were being treated by the accounting and shipping departments.

People just don't fit into molds. And what makes a complicated situation even more difficult is that they change. We cannot handle our people in convenient groupings; we must treat them as the personalities they are.

Many leaders have successfully avoided working *against* people. But that isn't enough. To really accomplish our goals, we must also avoid working *on* people and spend our time working *with* people.

In the materials handling field, a search was made for years for a material hard enough to stand up in the elbows of pipes pneumatically conveying sand; the abrasion would wear away the toughest material in just a few days. The solution to the problem was found when *rubber* was used as the wearing surface. It yielded—it gave—enough to resist being worn down. The analogy in working with the human element is a helpful one. Since we never really know what a person is thinking or feeling, we need to be pliable enough to change our direction or course of action when needed.

One of the great leaders of the American Revolution was Baron Von Steuben. During the terrible winter at Valley Forge, he wrote a complaining letter to a friend. He said that he always had to take time to tell Washington's soldiers *why* it was necessary that his orders be followed. But the tone of the Baron's letter changed to one of admiration, since he concluded that a lowly soldier's desire to know what was happening, and why, was the "genius of this nation." Most people want to know the score. In order to function most effectively for you, your subordinates and your co-workers need to be kept informed as to how things stand, how they got there and what you intend to do—and what part each of these people will play in that progress.

Whole libraries of books have been written on human

relations. What they tell you—some of them quite eloquently—boils down to just a few common-sense principles:

1. Treat each person as an individual.
2. Keep him informed.
3. Let him know where he stands.
4. Be genuinely appreciative of what he is and what he has done.
5. Provide opportunity for his growth and expression.
6. Be generous to him.
7. Behave in a way that he will respect.

It isn't necessary to getting some things done and making a success in life for many people to actually *like* you. But getting people to like you does make life sweeter and may well, as a side effect, make it possible for you to get still more done.

Summary

With the fundamentals behind you, improve your effectiveness with these techniques:

Take a fresh approach

Reduce to the absurd
Assume accomplishment
Distort time
Assume error
Assume another role
Identify with another
Mentally start over

Do it well.
Make use of your spare time.
Use your subconscious mind.
Use methods engineering principles.
Remember the human element.

11

USE TIME-SAVING
DEVICES

*Man is so made that he can only find relaxation
from one kind of labor by taking up another.*
— ANATOLE FRANCE

In addition to the general and basic requirements for getting more done, specific time-saving techniques are also
very helpful. Here are a dozen.

USE GRAPHIC SCHEDULING
AND PLANNING SYSTEMS

If you have a complex scheduling or staffing problem,
mount a large graphic system on a wall of your office. Many
of these devices are very clever in construction, with magnetic parts, pull-out tapes, movable cardboard or plastic
rectangles. Color-coding and specially-designed shapes add
to the interest value as well as to the interpretation.

It is much easier, of course, to comprehend a complex
situation when it is presented in graphical form rather than
as a series of names or numbers.

In staffing a large department, for example, a large

steel board can be mounted on an office wall. Colored adhesive tapes are used to lay out the organization of the department. Embossed plastic tapes indicate headings for buildings, work shifts or other categories.

Then, on magnetic strips, labels are affixed to indicate individual employee names. Colors can be used to indicate position (such as foreman, group leaders, etc.) or department. Special categories can be labeled to include names of people on sick leave, on vacation or otherwise unavailable for work. A blank would show a position open.

A similar board could be used for keeping track of construction progress for a new building, sales and quotas, production scheduling or other complicated or changing data.

CONTROL YOUR READING TIME

Do not fall into the trap of considering that any time spent at reading is of value to you. Many people spend well over an hour a day—seven days a week—reading the newspaper. This amounts to some ten weeks per year of equivalent work time! Yet, these same people will also listen to their favorite news programs on their car radios while riding to and from work and probably will also tune into the late evening television news. On top of all this may be piled a reading of a weekly news magazine!

Let me cast a challenge your way: stop reading the newspapers (perhaps it isn't even necessary to suggest watching less television). Give it a try for a month. Get your news from a periodical which you can read in much less total time; actually, most of the important news you'll be able to hear on the radio, perhaps in your car while driving. Newspapers are an attractive diversion, especially so since they are so well accepted socially. Remove the sensationalism, the advertising, manufactured news, cartoons, nonsense and special interest material and there isn't too much left. It would certainly be desirable to read that which is left, such as the editorials and a good deal of the material which normally occurs on the second page and a little bit of what appears on the front page, but it is hard to escape spending time on the adjacent material.

But if you do stop reading the newspapers, you will find yourself in an extremely small minority. Are you willing to try it?

LEARN TO READ
FASTER AND BETTER

Reading is simply a skill at which you can become very proficient, or you can perpetuate outmoded habits as long as you wish.

It is clear that the higher the executive position one attains, the larger the percentage of time one will spend in reading. Studies have shown that the typical executive can materially increase his reading speed while improving his comprehension of the printed matter.

Reading courses are now being taught in major cities by nationally represented firms. Courses are also being offered at both public schools and institutions of higher education, usually as evening classes. Correspondence courses are also available, as are books on the subject.

Of course, one should be able to read good literature carefully and with pleasure in the use of individual words but also be able to scan mountains of business printing rapidly.

When reading books, you naturally try to relate ideas to one another. But you should also attempt to relate books to each other. While reading, and again at completion, consider other books (not necessarily on a similar subject) and their relationship to the one at hand. It will help you in the evaluation of the new book, as well as give you a better insight into works you have read previously.

It's such a mistake to read a book and then forget it! What good is an experience you don't remember?

LET OTHERS READ FOR YOU

An organization can gain a great deal more from periodical literature if it is "farmed out." That is, let each person read a different group of periodicals, bringing to the attention of the balance of the group items of interest— he can even prepare synopses of them. It would be desirable to switch these reading responsibilities about every six months. Using such a system, you could give closer coverage to a larger number of publications.

If you are a plant manager, for example, there will be a number of magazines that will interest you but far too many for you to read personally. Let's assume that you have six management people reporting to you:

> Assistant Plant Manager
> Plant Engineer
> Production Manager
> Assistant Production Manager
> Traffic Manager
> Factory Superintendent

Each of these people should regularly read two or three periodicals that relate directly to his work. But in addition to this, you might prepare six categories of other periodicals, each category containing a few more periodicals. Then, assign a category to each person for a time and rotate quarterly or semi-annually. The rotation will provide a welcome change while tending to broaden the scope of your readers. Each person should remove or summarize articles of special interest, and send them to others who might be interested.

USE ABSTRACT OR
CLIPPING SERVICES

In order to expand the scope of current information coming to your attention, consider subscribing to abstract and excerpt services. A specialized type of service will send you clippings concerning almost any conceivable subject. You might wish to collect information on competitive companies or concerning a field you are considering entering through diversification. You might want to consider foreign as well as domestic sources, too.

USE SPECIALISTS
AND CONSULTANTS

Consider the use of consultants for knotty problems, especially where a rapid solution is desirable. Consider the cost and investment in time. It is typical that the consulting cost would be a lesser amount, in those special cases, than the cost of providing the same information or service internally.

As already mentioned, consulting fees are typically little higher than a company is paying its own people, all things considered. And, the specialist is not involved in spending time in familiarization with a specialized subject. He further has the benefit of experience and factual exchange on a broad basis, rather than within a single organization. He can provide an objective approach without being hampered by preconceived limitations of tradition or personality.

The consultant holds up a mirror so that the client may look in to see himself as he *is*. The consultant also provides a conscience, a stimulus for action.

About two thousand firms are engaged in some form of consulting on a full-time basis. Their business volume is probably approaching a half-billion dollars annually. Consultants are used both to solve known problems and to define and solve suspected problems. Although management may seek aid in reaching decisions, it should not—it cannot —abdicate its prerogatives by expecting a consultant to make its decisions.

If you are considering the use of a consultant, find out these things from him:

1. His experience with problems like yours
2. The time schedule, starting and ending dates
3. Names and qualifications of the people who will actually do the work
4. References
5. A firm proposal with options if desired

By all means, avoid "bargains." Seek a real value by finding a capable consultant whose personality will best fit in with your people.

USE TEMPLATES AND MODELS

If you work with buildings, machinery, layouts and other physical things, use templates for the simpler items and three-dimensional models for the more complex items. They can prevent serious errors and omissions and assure that everyone is thinking or talking about the same thing.

There are now companies that manufacture both templates and models in various scales. Plastic drawing templates (like stencils) make it easy to lay out office furniture, homes, fixtures, rail lines, machinery.

Models are invariably used for complex chemical process installations, if for nothing more than to assure that the piping layout is economical and will work. Clear plastic sheets can be used to simulate floors in multi-story buildings so that both horizontal and vertical alignment can be checked.

MAKE REGULAR USE OF
A TICKLER FILE

Get in the habit of using a tickler file every day. You can handle it personally, or you can turn it over to a secretary or clerk. It will assure you of not letting something slip by that should be handled within a certain deadline. Even things that should be done monthly, for example, can be placed in the tickler file on the same day of each month. Some people substitute a calendar pad, but this is not handy for actually inserting the material which should be referred to on a given date.

The tickler file is simply a series of dividers or folders,

one marked for each day of the month, one for each month of the year. Items are placed in the tickler so that they will come to your attention when you next desire. The only requirement is that you check the proper divider every day.

The tickler makes working with a clear desk easy since everything that cannot be handled during the work day can be placed in the tickler for the next day or some future date. If an item is too bulky, it can be placed in a storage cabinet and a reminder can be put in the tickler file.

MAKE GREATER USE OF
THE TELEPHONE

Make more use of the telephone. Instead of writing a letter or walking to another office or calling a meeting, use the telephone. Even long-distance calls can be much more eonomical than exchanging a series of letters and certainly are quicker.

Local telephone companies are anxious to be of service in helping you use the telephone most effectively. They have valuable publications on the subject and can also give you consultation. And, communications consultants are also available.

Sometimes it's neither a matter of time nor expense. Some salesmen use the long-distance telephone merely because of the psychological impact. To many people, a long distance call is "important business."

ARRANGE YOUR WORK AREA

Don't waste a lot of time in unnecessary travel from one part of the room to another or even from one side of your desk to the other. Organize the desk itself—why keep it crowded with materials you rarely use? Put often-used items within easy reach. From your chair, with no more than a turning motion, you should be able to reach:

> All areas of your desk
> A side or back table
> Communications equipment
> Dictation equipment
> Waste basket
> File cabinet, bucket or drawer
> Other things you might use regularly, such as a radio, calculator, typewriter, books

WRITE SHORTER LETTERS

Get in the habit of writing shorter letters. Enlist the aid of your secretary and ask her to remove extraneous or duplicated material. Many people's letters are much more flowery than their conversation; they would do much better to write as if they were speaking in person to the receiver. Half-size and two-thirds size letterheads and post cards help to control this short-letter discipline.

Let's look at Lincoln's *complete letter* to Governor Curtin of Pennsylvania, written on April 8, 1861, on the eve of the Civil War: "I think the necessity of being *ready* increases—Look to it."

The letter conveys information of the gravest nature. But Lincoln didn't make the mistake of confusing the length of a letter with its importance. We should all know that a reader is going to give a certain total amount of attention to a letter; the longer the letter, the less attention is going to be given to any one thought in it. The really important subjects require *short* letters with the emphasis properly placed so that the real thought cannot be lost.

Of all the mail I have ever received, I can remember the exact contents of only two letters.

From a friend and mentor:

That was a good article you wrote.

From an uncle:

Thinking of you in Chicago.

There is no question of why they wrote the letters or what they felt. Anything written in addition would have diluted their content.

Try answering at least one letter a day with a single sentence, perhaps something like these:

I thought the enclosed data would interest you.

I'm looking forward to seeing you next Tuesday morning.

News of your honor made me happy. Congratulations!

Your last order was appreciated; may we be of service again?

We would appreciate your calling on us when you are next in this area.

Regretfully, we are unable to supply the information you seek.

WORK FROM CHECK LISTS

Work from check lists when dealing with a subject which involves a large number of factors. They can save embarrassing or costly mistakes such as the construction of a multi-story building without elevators (it has been done). Some people pack their suitcases from a check list— it's not as silly as it sounds, you'll agree, when you find yourself away from home with no neckties. In addition to being memory aides, check lists can also serve as stimuli to thought.

The check list can contain only a dozen items, such as the major factors to be included in a contract. Or, it can be a detailed list hundreds of pages long, such as is used for hospital construction planning.

"You can't get there from here" isn't always a funny punch line. It was just simply true when the planners of a major highway intersection failed to provide a linkage for two of the lanes. A check list may be superfluous sometimes, but it can sometimes pay off very well.

SUMMARY

Use these twelve special techniques to get more done:

Use graphic scheduling and planning systems.
Control your reading time.
Learn to read faster and better.
Let others read for you.
Use abstract or clipping services.
Use specialists and consultants.
Use templates and models.
Make regular use of a tickler file.
Make greater use of the telephone.
Arrange your work area.
Get in the habit of writing shorter letters.
Work from check lists.

12

ANOTHER DOZEN TECHNIQUES

A man's work is in danger of deteriorating when he thinks he has found the one best formula for doing it. If he thinks that, he is likely to feel that all he needs is merely to go on repeating himself. . . . So long as a person is searching for better ways of doing his work he is fairly safe.

—EUGENE O'NEILL

SET TIME LIMITS ON INTERVIEWS AND CONFERENCES

The length of interviews can be controlled by setting a time limit in advance. Some people actually use an alarm clock, but this is rather harsh. Merely inform the caller of the time at which the interview must end because of other business or set up a system whereby your secretary calls, say, ten minutes after a visitor has entered your office. You have the option of terminating the conversation ostensibly because of the call or continuing it if you desire. Bear in mind that the shortening of interview time is a service to the caller when you have no serious interest in the

169

subject. However, courtesy to the caller and attentiveness to his words are absolutely required.

Where a time limit is set for an interview, the caller is required to either state his case in that time or arouse enough interest to gain more time through an extension of the interview or the setting of another appointment. This means that he cannot afford to spend much time on things that don't count. He will minimize the warm-up or getting acquainted period so that he can concentrate on his exposition of facts or demonstrations. He will want to save time, too, for meeting any objections you might come up with. Only if he has time to spare in closing will he tell jokes, relate anecdotes or discuss mutual acquaintances. Thus, your impression will be of facts and his ability to handle them rather than of his personality.

Limiting conferences has the same effect. Extraneous material is simply omitted because there isn't time for it.

USE MORE FORM LETTERS

See that your organization uses more form letters. With the use of the automatic typewriter, these can be made to look like any other letters if this is desired. The federal government, for example, makes good use of check-off letters which contain boxes to be marked for indication of applicable parts of the letters, the balance to be ignored.

A purchasing department, for example, should rarely have to write an original letter. The same would be true of a traffic department, a credit department and a customer service department (incidentally, in the last case, telephone calls—and certainly including long distance—should be utilized far more frequently to establish a personal contact and to make certain of satisfying the customer's wishes).

The following is a form letter that might be used by a purchasing department. With the use of such a form, only a relatively few individual letters would have to be written. (Note that all typing is done on the same margin setting.)

JONES-SMITH COMPANY

(Purchasing Department Form Letter)

Please feel free to make your response on this form, if convenient.

Date   :
To   :
Address   :
Order No. :
Invoice   :
B/L No. :

☐ Your estimated delivery date was ....
When will delivery actually be made?
☐ Please indicate price and delivery on the following:

☐ Please deliver this order for the following:

☐ Please identify carrier and B/L number.
☐ Please cancel our order.
☐ Please remove the following from our order:

☐ Please add the following to our order:

☐ Please expedite delivery. Items urgently needed.

☐ Please indicate shipping date.
☐ The following items were missing from your shipment. Please forward right away.

☐ The following items were received damaged. Please forward replacements and provide disposition of damaged items.
☐ Other:

Thank you,

Al Thompson, P. A.

CLEAR YOUR DESK

To some people, a cluttered desk signifies a cluttered mind. (No, an empty desk doesn't indicate an empty mind!) Consider keeping on your desk only the materials which might be worked on *today*. Everything else can go into various categories: to the tickler file for the next day or some future date; to your home for leisure reading; in the waste basket where unquestionably a great deal of it should go; in the files. Further, at the end of the day it is good practice to remove everything, putting materials into the categories already named, clearing the desk as well as the mind for the next day's work (and, incidentally, providing some good housekeeping at the same time).

Undoubtedly, there is much to this subject that has to do with personality. Literary people seem to be inclined toward surrounding themselves with printed matter. I know of one scientist (a brilliant man) who has all the furniture in his office so covered with books, letters, files and other items that he sits on the floor to do much of his work. There he works, surrounded by concentric circles of materials piled around him.

Some people actually are able to use this "system" as a method of handy filing; their unusual memories make it possible for them to know what information they possess and where it is. But for most people, it represents a failure at organization and puts a severe limit on their effectiveness.

WORK WHILE TRAVELING

Save certain types of work to be done while traveling. There is at least one author, for example, who deliberately takes trains on occasion so as to be sure of gaining several uninterrupted hours of writing time, using a small portable dictating machine.

Traveling is stimulating; new faces, conversation, places and situations bring fresh ideas. And one brings along only those things that he intends to work with—no distracting telephone calls and visitors. A motel room, albeit a lonesome place, is a good environment for productive work—cool, quiet, providing all the necessities without undue disturbance.

VISUALIZE YOUR IDEAS

Get used to using visual means of selling your ideas. A number of very good kits are available for making graphs and charts—containing grid papers with title blocks, adhesive tapes of various designs and colors for making lines and the like.

Consider regular use of one or more of these aids to visualization:

Chalkboard
Newsprint pad with crayon, grease pencil or felt
    ink markers
Poster board with adhesive markers
Grid paper
Colored construction paper
Models
Maps
Layout schematics

A hospital with less than a hundred beds is no organizational giant but it is complicated enough to present a number of problems. There may be a hundred or more employees who must provide varying levels of coverage three shifts a day, seven days a week. Occupancy of the patient rooms (with from one to four people per room) is very important, since it determines income; yet the institution may be made of a collection of wings and areas in a complex layout. Future expansion must be carefully considered.

An intelligent, hard-working administrator in a situation like this found that his ability to handle all the details of scheduling and room utilization was becoming less and less effective as his hospital grew; he was trying to handle it all by himself without visual aids.

The answer to his problem was the installation of two devices in his office. On one wall he mounted a magnetic organization board so he could keep track of all assignments on a daily basis; on another wall he mounted a layout of his building, showing the bed capacity of each room, so he could assure himself of the highest possible occupancy (consistent with good patient care). And, the schematic also indicated the property lines so he could use it for planning purposes.

Visual systems tend to take a lot of concern out of a day's work, even if the results were to turn out to be the same.

USE A CHALKBOARD

A chalkboard mounted on one wall of your office is a very handy working tool. It permits you and others to depict ideas that could only otherwise be verbalized. You can use it for making a continuous check list, adding and taking off items as need be. The board should be at least six feet long (eight or ten feet is better), and the center of the board should be at the height of *your* shoulder.

The green boards are more attractive and actually easier on the eyes than the black boards. Although colored chalk is helpful for complicated drawings or lists, its use should be minimized since the clay binder tends to "load" the surface of the board, leaving "ghosts" and slick spots. Chalkboards should be dry cleaned daily with a plain cotton cloth or plastic sponge and washed or damp cleaned only periodically; daily applications of water tend to ruin a board.

Here are some ways chalkboards can be used successfully:

> Listing of salesmen, quotas and shipments
> Listing of clients, last date visited and next visit due
> Listing of service men, location and date due to return to office
> Listing of orders, shipment date and status
> Sketching for design work
> Memory aids
> In-and-out register

Forms design
Name and slogan development

Sometimes it's desirable to put permanent markings on chalkboards so that each time the board is erased, the material doesn't have to be redrawn. One can use paint or plastic tape to provide lines and boxes; a building plan can be painted on with the use of each area shown in chalk.

KEEP A TIME LOG

Try keeping a daily time log. Every time you change from one thing to another, put it down on the sheet. Do this for a week or so, then analyze all the sheets together. Determine what percentage of your time is being spent on each of your various types of duties.

Depending on your type of work, you might develop a listing somewhat like the following, put it on a columnar data pad and keep your time to the nearest quarter hour:

Contact with superiors
Contact with co-workers
Contact with subordinates
Interviewing salesmen
Planning
Handling correspondence
Telephone calls, incoming
Transportation
Direct supervision
Inspections
Personal
Research, investigation
Forms and reports

Meetings
Scheduling work
Other (identify)

Although it may not be apparent on a daily basis, such a time log can show, over a period of time, undue emphasis on some functions and not enough on others. You will probably want to make some changes!

USE STANDARD PARAGRAPHS

Make use of standard paragraphs in your correspondence. These can be set up initially by going back through a hundred or so carbons of letters and clipping out paragraphs containing subjects which seem to occur with some regularity. Edit each of these paragraphs so that they are shorter and perhaps read even better than when first written. Organize them into subject categories (such as "P" for purchasing, "A" for administrative, "L" for legal, etc.) and number the paragraphs under each section. After the number, provide an identification for the paragraph in one or two words, such as "when can we expect shipment," or "my next visit." The paragraphs can have blanks in them for filling in dates, names or numbers. Using standard paragraphs, a letter might be *dictated* as follows:

Dear Mr. Jones:

P-3 (5152)
A-1 (January 15)
A-15, Mr. Jones
B-4

Cordially yours,

From the above, the typist would prepare the following letter:

Dear Mr. Jones:

We are grateful for your order number 5152. As you know, the increasing interest in variable speed drives has taxed our productive capacity rather heavily, as it has other manufacturers of this type equipment.

Nevertheless, we expect to make delivery to you on or before January 15. We sincerely hope this date will not inconvenience you in any way.

Since we established our engineering trouble-shooting department last year, our specialists have visited twenty-three plants and have assisted their managements in solving twenty-seven transmission problems. We are anxious to serve you in this unique way, too, Mr. Jones!

Won't you stop in at our booth at the forthcoming Plant Engineering Show? We'll be showing the very latest in transmission equipment, and it's always good to see old friends!

Cordially yours,

The time to consider the use of standard paragraphs is when, as you're dictating, it occurs to you that you've heard those words before!

LET YOUR SECRETARY
SAVE YOU TIME

Your secretary can save time for you in these and
other ways:

1. It is not necessary for you to compose every letter
from beginning to end—let her keep a few sample letters
and from that point on, just give her the ideas, dates and
events, and let her take it from there.

2. Let her screen the people who want to call on you
and talk with you, and let her set up your appointment
calendar. Of course, it is best to set limits on this and to
leave yourself a certain flexibility, such as leaving one
period free each day or only making appointments during
that period each day.

3. She can handle your filing, library, supplies, even
your own desk organization.

4. Let her take care of meetings, conferences and
various events and make all the arrangements involved in
them.

5. Give your secretary your travel plans and let her
take care of obtaining tickets, lodging, letters of confirma-
tion, assembling files and collecting pertinent data.

6. Let her screen and organize your mail (although
some people seem to get a special kick out of opening their
own mail).

CONTROL YOUR PAPER WORK

The savings available to most organizations in each of these categories of paperwork can be astonishing:

1. Correspondence, both formal and informal. Limit the number of carbon copies sent; question any letter over one page in length; use short letterhead forms; use post cards; use form letters; reply on the same letter.

2. Filing. Do not assume that everything has to be filed; use microfilm where applicable; use open filing where applicable; separate live files from storage files.

3. Forms. Simplify the forms; keep to one side of one page only; avoid legal size forms; if carbons must be used, try to avoid separate carbon pages; eliminate the need for writing by using check-off boxes; combine forms to eliminate some of them.

4. Records. Eliminate unnecessary records; establish a discard date; set conditions which will cause discontinuance.

5. Reports. Question any report more than one page in length; use graphs and charts; reduce the number of copies involved; check the frequency.

6. Literature. Circulate magazines, advertising matter and other incoming or organization-created literature only to interested parties; send stop notices to companies regularly sending unwanted literature.

Issue stickers which can be used for the discontinuance of forms or listings where they are not required by the receiver.

Set up a ruling that requires the initiator of every item to maintain the permanent file, where required, in a location accessible to everyone so the recipients can discard their copies without fear of a permanent copy being unavailable. Carbon copies require time for:

> A secretary to handle and mail.
> A mail clerk to route.
> A secretary to receive.
> A receiver to read.
> Disposal.

Consider appointing an individual within the organization to coordinate cost-improvement activities in paperwork control. Approval would have to be received from this person before any new forms were printed, and all such forms would have to carry his control number. He would make suggestions for combining forms, condensing and eliminating them.

USE AN EMPIRICAL APPROACH

Do not be afraid to use an empirical approach. Perhaps you have heard the legend of the scientist in Edison's laboratory trying to work out the formula for calculating the volume of a light bulb of complex shape; Edison merely filled it with water, then poured the water into a graduated beaker. (This is similar to the cook's trick of measuring a half-cup of butter by filling a cup half full of water, then adding butter until the cup is filled.)

Use approximations where they will serve the purpose. To calculate the thickness of metal to be used for a certain noncritical component, for example, it may be cheaper to have a tradesman make a mock-up in several sample thicknesses and test them to destruction than having engineers and scientists work on the job in a laboratory or at a computer. The correct answer may be found at one-tenth the cost (and besides, you would probably insist on testing out the theoretical answer anyhow).

This is not to say that the empirical approach is uniformly better than a calculated approach—of course not. But there are times when approximation by trial and error can give adequate results at a much lesser cost. In this day of computers and teams of scientists and engineers, we tend to forget the simpler ways of doing things.

There's an old, sarcastic saying in the chemical industry, often repeated by people who are responsible for preparing product labels: "When all else fails, read the directions." Perhaps we are in the same state with respect to our technology, but I hope we won't wait for our complex, expensive methods of problem solving to fail before we try the empirical approach.

WORK STANDING UP

People work faster when they are somewhat uncomfortable than they do in more pleasant situations. (Perhaps you noticed this in school when studying—you may have done better on a test after studying in a cool room than you did after studying in a warm room.)

Many people have come to find that working on their feet gets so many more things done that they prefer to use the old-fashioned standing desk and actually remove the chairs from their office for at least part of the day. Perhaps you would like to start an experiment in this direction by standing up the latter half of the day, when you are more apt to slow down.

It's true that standing is more fatiguing than sitting,

but the increased productivity is worth it. Sitting down actually becomes a self-reward for completed work!

Perhaps this all sounds a bit ludicrous to you, but, nevertheless, it works for many people. Don't you think it deserves at least a try?

CONSIDER EVERY OCCURRENCE AS AN OPPORTUNITY

Consider every occurrence, every change, as an opportunity. At the least, it is an opportunity to take action that may have been formerly blocked but is now possible because of the occurrence. But in the more general sense, change provides the opportunity for re-evaluation. Let's say that a key executive has resigned. The typical first order of business, lamentation, should be avoided, as should recrimination. First, evaluate the situation to determine why the key man left and then determine if steps to prevent recurrence are feasible or desirable. Then, re-examine the organization or department involved. Maybe this is the chance you have been waiting for to promote a promising young man, to make a desirable transfer, to reorganize so that there are more "Indians" and less "chiefs," to eliminate a function or service, to shift or reassign responsibilities or even to take over the function yourself. When every occurrence is considered a crisis rather than an opportunity, organization is weakened rather than strengthened.

Let's eavesdrop on a conversation between a sales manager and a company president:

SALES MANAGER: This is going to hurt; we've lost the Golding account.

PRESIDENT: That *is* rough. Wasn't that Brewster's biggest account?

SALES MANAGER: It sure was—I guess it made up over half of his volume. He'll have a heck of a time replacing it; he hasn't gotten a new account in months.

PRESIDENT: You know, maybe this is a blessing in disguise. I remember you told me that Brewster was a marginal man, and if he hadn't brought over the Golding account with him, you never would have hired him.

SALES MANAGER: Yes, that's true. As a matter of fact, he never did make much money for us, so I guess we haven't lost anything after all. We can drop him and distribute his remaining customers among our other men in this area. It will give them a good boost, particularly at this time of year, and serve the customers better, also.

PRESIDENT: There's another benefit from this, too. Golding is the firm we are making that special product for; it takes special materials and special equipment. Now, we can drop it and save ourselves space and inventory.

SALES MANAGER: Well, I guess it wasn't such a bad happening after all.

PRESIDENT: Frankly, what I'm thinking now is that there may be other cases like this and that we shouldn't wait for something to happen to take action on them.

SALES MANAGER: I'll make up a list of marginal men and special products, and we'll look into them.

Opportunities from apparently damaging occurrences may not appear so readily as in the above case, but at least every occurrence should be searched for possible benefits.

SUMMARY

These additional useful devices can be put to work to save you time.

Set time limits in advance on interviews and conferences.
Use more form letters.
Clear your desk.
Do certain types of work while traveling.
Visualize your ideas.
Use a chalkboard.
Keep a daily time log for a while.
Make use of standard paragraphs in correspondence.
Let your secretary save you time.
Control your paper work.
Do not be afraid to use an empirical approach.
Work standing up.
Consider every occurrence as an opportunity.

13

SPECIAL TECHNIQUES ARE HELPFUL

I find that the harder I work, the luckier I get.
—Lyndon Johnson

With the foundation of the previous chapters to build on, let's take a look at some individual time-saving and result-producing ideas. This will also provide an opportunity to review some earlier ideas that will be worked in. The random order is deliberate, not only to demonstrate the wide variety of techniques that you can use but also to stimulate your thinking about them.

ANSWER ON THE PIECE RECEIVED

A letter is usually an invitation, stated or not, for another letter to be written in return. Even the statement "no reply required" doesn't always finish the exchange.

Write your reply to a letter or inter-office communication directly on the original piece. Since there probably won't be too much room left, or since you may be writing in longhand, you will be sure to keep your reply short! And, it has the touch of finality about it and thus is not likely to provoke a response. You see, if there will be another letter from the original sender, he must start all over again rather than just continue the original correspondence.

There are other advantages to sending back the original letter with your answer written on it. First, it directly relates the answer to the letter, and the receiver doesn't have to match them up. (If there is really going to be an exchange of ideas, the same material can be sent back and forth several times, with new ideas added on each sending.) Then, the procedure avoids dictation, typing and proofing time. Finally, it provides a personal touch. (Some people have a good time sending the same birthday card back and forth through the mails year after year; the pretext is economy, but it really indicates a personal interest.)

CONDUCT A MEETING WITHOUT CHAIRS

If you are having difficulty with meetings lasting too long, conduct the next one in a room which has no chairs. As ridiculous as this sounds, it works. People do not ramble when they are on their tired feet—they get to the point. The things of importance will be discussed, and the trivia will be omitted. Your meeting will be conducted in half the time; yet the *important* business will have been transacted.

It may not be necessary that this be done regularly. But, periodically, it does have the benefit of demonstrating, in a memorable way, the cost of conducting meetings and just how little time really needs to be spent in order to cover only the points of business.

TRY A BRAIN-STORMING SESSION

There is absolutely no substitute for the individual human mind when it comes to solving problems or creating new ideas. But we can use supplementary techniques, and one of these is "brain-storming." Like most things that have met with success, though, the technique has been over-used and mis-used and for some people has gotten a bad name. This shouldn't keep us from using it where it will be helpful.

The purpose of brain-storming is to put a number of people in such a controlled situation that they will develop a large *quantity* of ideas; the ideas are later sorted through by others and evaluated for possible use. It's like asking a group of neighbors for help in shaking the fruit from an apple tree; once their combined strength has brought many apples to the ground, you then have to sort them through to eliminate those that cannot be used.

The participants must not be inhibited; there must be strict rules against humor and sarcasm; there must be no attempt to judge or evaluate ideas while they are being thrown out—they are merely to be listed. There must be as little distraction as possible. The use of a tape recorder running the full length of the session will eliminate the need for writing or even for starting and stopping the machine.

If you've reached a dead end in your thinking and need some new ideas or stimulation, consider a brain-storming session. Get a group of a half-dozen people together—advance notice doesn't help—and have the recorder and the room all ready for them. Tell them the nature of the problem, reassure them that there will be no judgments and encourage them to go "far out." If you don't come up with a specific idea, you might at least have suggested a direction for investigation.

Let's drop in on a session being held in the office of the personnel manager of a manufacturing company. He has asked people with various backgrounds to help him brain-storm the problem of excessive absenteeism in the service force. The session is already in progress. . . .

> FOREMAN: This is a highly mechanized plant
> —*except* for service people. Make their
> work more mechanical; get them more ma-
> chinery to work with.
>
> SALES MANAGER: Everybody likes recogni-
> tion. Post notices in each area of the plant
> to show who's responsible for its upkeep.
>
> ENGINEER: And give an award for the best-
> maintained area of the month.
>
> SALES MANAGER: Sure, publicize the win-
> ner in the paper.
>
> TRAFFIC MANAGER: I'd fine them for ex-
> cessive absenteeism.
>
> ENGINEER: Pay a bonus at the end of each
> month for perfect attendance.
>
> FOREMAN: Or give a day of paid vacation.
>
> TRAFFIC MANAGER: All their equipment
> looks bad—paint it up.
>
> SALES MANAGER: Maybe it's their super-
> visors; get them into a training program.
>
> SUPERINTENDENT: Why not training for the
> workers themselves—that helps morale, and
> good morale limits absenteeism.
>
> FOREMAN: Maybe more of it is medical than
> we think; maybe there's some kind of dis-

ease going around that we don't know about.

ENGINEER: Maybe the smell from the new process is driving them off—it sure makes *me* sick.

TRAFFIC MANAGER: How about a family day so everyone can see the place. Getting the plant spruced up should keep everybody interested for a month.

FOREMAN: We've been too easy on them. I'd fire everybody with excessive absenteeism. That would stop it.

SALES MANAGER: Maybe we're in the wrong part of the country—move somewhere else.

SUPERINTENDENT: Maybe it's the wrong kind of business—not romantic and all, what with rockets all over the place.

FOREMAN: Maybe just one aerospace contract would make a difference. . . .

ENGINEER: Why not poll our employees to ask them what the trouble is?

SUPERINTENDENT: Or hire a consultant to find out.

FOREMAN: Put an undercover man on the payroll to find out.

SALES MANAGER: Could be the pay. Maybe we can automate more and pay the people who stay a higher rate.

SUPERINTENDENT: Maybe there's some sort of interesting thing going on that's keeping the workers away, maybe gambling or something.

FOREMAN: Maybe they're job hunting.

SALES MANAGER: They don't feel part of

the organization. The plant manager should have meetings with them regularly.

TRAFFIC MANAGER: Maybe the union is doing this deliberately.

ENGINEER: Management should. . . .

And on and on the ideas come. There was no rebuttal, no criticism, no making fun. The problem was approached from both a constructive and corrective standpoint with no effort made to channelize thought. And, maybe, the personnel manager will get what he needs from the brainstorming session. But the final decision—the final action recommended—must be his alone, as an individual.

USE POST CARDS

Unfortunately, use of the post card is diminishing as a means of communication. That's too bad from a business standpoint, since it can save so much time and money. Perhaps it's just a phase we're going through, and all that is needed for its revival is regular use by some of our larger companies.

The post card has many advantages:

1. Eliminates cost of envelope.
2. Cheaper than letterhead.
3. Less postage.
4. No time involved in folding, stuffing, sealing and stamping.
5. The smaller size invites shorter correspondence.
6. No time required for opening.

The post card may be a form letter in itself, with check-off boxes and fill-in spaces. It may be provided to a receiver as a form reply card. It may be a perforated section of a brochure or magazine page.

Post cards can be printed to include your company letterhead in miniature, a multi-color trademark or a complete form message and signature. You might even consider having some printed for your personal use.

USE YOUR SUBCONSCIOUS MIND

Deliberately make use of your subconscious mind. There is no longer any doubt that we can put our subconscious to work on problems which it can solve better than our conscious mind. Once the facts have been obtained and committed to memory, consider the problem consciously and then "forget it" for a while. You will have let the mind bubble and sparkle with conscious thought, then simmer and steep with subconscious thought. But be prepared with pencil and paper, because the solution to your problem may boil to the surface at a most unexpected time! Warning: if the subconscious fails to work, be sure you have enough time left to solve the problem in the usual way!

USE SPECIAL CORRESPONDENCE DEVICES

We have already discussed writing answers onto the message received, form letters and post cards. Correspondence deserves still more discussion; a tremendous amount of time is consumed in this activity.

Much of what we do with respect to correspondence is due to custom and fashion. If we can change some of those customs and fashions, we can save a great deal of time and money.

Let's take the window envelope for example. It is a very clever idea: it avoids the retyping of the address, since the one on the letter itself shows through. But people associate window envelopes with bills and third-class mail. When we can begin to use it for first class mail—there is no reason other than custom against it—we will reap great savings and even eliminate numerous errors in transcription.

We can go on a step further. The envelope itself is a rather recent device; formerly, the letter was merely folded and sealed, and the address written on the back. You may recall the "Victory Mail" of World War II. The letter folded to make its own envelope; removing a perforated edging opened the letter. There is no reason—other than custom—this could not be done in business. We could even take it further: the address could fold to the outside and have on it a printed stamp. The receiver would have a letter with the address, stamp and post mark on the upper third and the body of the letter below. The lower third might even contain the reply area.

In time, all correspondence paper may be sensitized in some way so that "carbons" may be made without the use of separate carbon papers or without the need for relatively expensive coatings on the paper. When this occurs, we can eliminate both carbon papers and envelopes, reducing fire hazards along with the big custodial cost of waste removal.

REDUCE THE NUMBER OF REPORT COPIES

In order to reduce the number of copies of reports which are distributed, or even possibly to eliminate the report completely, stop sending them out (unless management has determined beyond any doubt that they are indeed indispensable). See who complains about not receiving the items and investigate these complaints. Strike the others off the list.

The odds are you will have kept on your distribution list only the few people who are really interested and removed a number of recipients who really didn't care. You may even find that no one cares, and the entire report can be eliminated! At the least, you will save time in the preparation, distribution and filing of some copies.

USE COLOR-CODING

Do not overlook the advantages of color-coding. More and more items are being color-coded these days, from grades of lumber to file folders, because it saves time and eliminates errors in identification.

A major project, for example, could be designated "operation red," and everything connected with it marked in the red color. Each month, or each fiscal period, could be given a distinctive color. Color flags can indicate past-due accounts, urgent status or priority. Color pins can indicate location of salesmen, accounts, trouble spots, vacant territories.

Caution: watch out for color blind people!

ANNOUNCE THE AGENDA FOR A MEETING

Perhaps you have had this experience: you have been called to attend a meeting, you arrive and sit down with a dozen other people. After twenty minutes of conversation, someone finally asks, "By the way, what are we here for?"

To get the most good out of a meeting or conference, announce in advance the subjects for discussion and distribute statistical or other pertinent information at least a day before the event. Then, when the actual meeting begins, restate its purpose and be sure everyone understands it.

While we're on the subject of meetings, let's list some things that make meetings more productive while making them shorter:

1. Again, announce the purpose of the meeting.
2. Distribute pertinent data in advance.
3. Name the chairman; if he may be absent, have a substitute named.
4. Invite only the people necessary to the meeting's success. If you merely want to inform people, don't mix that purpose with a developmental session; handle it separately.
5. Be sure that the discussions remain impersonal and objective.
6. Check out the suggested time and place to be sure that it doesn't work an unusual hardship on some of the attendees.
7. If possible, set a time limit and adjourn at that time; thus, the attendees can make plans for the balance of the day.
8. Get right to the point; leave the stories and pleasantries for other times and places. But, of course, this does not mean the absence of humor from the discussions.
9. Permit only one person to speak at a time; use rules of order.
10. Provide note pads and pencils.
11. If it must be a very long meeting, require

a short break every hour for personal reasons.

If you happen to be the chairman, you can help the meeting achieve its intended results in these ways:

1. Listen carefully to what is said, while keeping all remarks centered on the stated problem.
2. Look for similar ideas which may have been
   expressed in different ways and point out
   their agreement.
3. Where opinions differ, attempt to reconcile
   them.
4. When creative ideas are expressed, under-
   score them and try to expand them, taking
   other ideas in where possible.
5. Clarify any statements that seem ambiguous;
   example or analogy can be helpful.
6. Periodically, make a step-by-step re-evaluation of progress made toward the solution of
   the problem.
7. Finally, restate the accepted solution to be
   sure that there is either accord or that no objections have been unanswered.

WRITE DOWN YOUR THOUGHTS

Of course, it is desirable to write down ideas when they occur simply to keep them from being lost, but writing things down can be helpful beyond this.

For one thing, it requires you to organize your thoughts. Things can go around in your head in an amorphous form, but as soon as you begin to commit those thoughts to paper, you find the need to arrange them in an orderly way. It has often been said, if you want to learn a given subject, write an article or a book about it! It will require you to research the subject as well as to arrange the material in a logical form and thus learn it.

Writing ideas out can point out areas of information weakness, and it can help you to apply a title or slogan to the work.

MAKE PROPER USE OF THE DICTATING MACHINE

Where a person does a good deal of correspondence or writing, the only excuse for failure to use a dictating machine should be the need for a "sounding board," for those people who function more effectively when able to get ideas from a competent secretary. Legitimate examples of this should be quite rare.

Good dictation technique can save your secretary time, prevent errors, avoid having to do work over and assure you of the shortest proofing time. In its brochure "How to be a Dictator," the Stenocord Corporation provides rules for good dictation technique:

Rule One

TELL HER WHAT IT IS:

A Letter
Inter-office Memo
Report
Rough Draft

Wire
Form Number

ON WHAT KIND OF PAPER:

Company Letterhead
Personal Stationery
Second Sheets
Onion Skin
Etc.

Rule Two

TELL HER THE NUMBER OF COPIES

Say, "An original and three carbons"

AND THE TYPE OF PAPER:

Bond
Onion Skin
Etc.

Rule Three

NAME OF THE PERSON:
Spell it out. *Henry K. B-u-t-t-e-r-f-i-
-e-l-d*

Rule Four

NAME OF THE COMPANY
NUMBER AND STREET
CITY

STATE
ZIP CODE

Rule Five

SEPARATE IDEAS:
Paragraph 1 . . .
Paragraph 2 . . .
Paragraph 3 . . .

Rule Six

CALL PARAGRAPHS:
Dictate each paragraph around your key word or idea—
Then say—"Period paragraph"

Rule Seven

PUNCTUATION:
With 34 rules for and against the use of commas, the simplest one to remember is to say COMMA, specifically where you want the reader to pause!

Rule Eight

MECHANICS:
Quotes
Say "Open quote"
Make quotation
Say "Close quote"
Parenthesis
Say "Open parenthesis" [or "Open paren"]
Include matter apart from main thought

Say "Close parenthesis"

Indentations

"Please indent the next paragraph x number of spaces."

Columns

Here you must visualize what you want and then tell her "Reading from left to right set up columns as follows."

[Or attach a sketch]

Sub Paragraphs

"Please indent the next sub paragraphs using small letters or numbers."

Rule Nine

FORMS:

Dictate all printed forms such as applications for insurance claims, inventory and ruled forms of all kinds, from left to right and top to bottom, by filling in the necessary information. These are the easiest.

But keep a blank copy of the form in front of you while dictating.

VARY YOUR RATE OF SPEECH

Ever think of talking faster? You can actually talk a good deal faster, if you consciously think about doing so, and can certainly be just as well understood—perhaps even more so in most cases. This is not to say that we all should try to be like the amazing Floyd Gibbons, but we might decide that we haven't got time to indulge in a drawl!

We may solve some of our communications problems, too, by adjusting our speech rate to the individual to whom we are speaking. You would naturally want to speak faster to a "sharp" person, in order to be able to hold his attention; if you talk too slowly to him, you will lose him. On the other hand, there are people to whom you should speak more slowly, so that you do not lose them. They may actually be just as intelligent as the other man but not able to handle verbal material as fast.

When was the last time you consciously regulated your rate of speaking?

ADVERTISE YOUR BUYING AS WELL AS SELLING

If you are involved in buying, why not "advertise" just as you would when trying to sell something. For example, post a list of wanted items, along with the prices you are willing to pay for these items (you can determine what savings you must enjoy before you are willing to change vendors and use this for selecting the figures). Show samples of the items—or a mock-up, if samples have not been manufactured. Indicate the estimated or guaranteed quantities over a given period of time. Such posted information will save you, and some of the vendors calling on you, a great deal of time while helping to achieve improved costs.

PROVIDE CALLERS AND VISITORS WITH LITERATURE

Literature made available to people who call on you can save your people time in explaining. It can also give you the public relations benefit of saving your callers time, too.

Your visitor's booklet should be posted in a conspicuous place and might contain:

1. A schematic plan of the premises, so people can find their way about.

2. A listing of names and titles of the people most often called on, their whereabouts and telephone numbers.

3. Security and other regulations, such as smoking, safety glasses, etc.

4. Promotional material about the organization, its products or services, its history and aims.

5. A listing of functions or items and the person to see in each case.

6. A listing of affiliated or subsidiary organizations, their product and location.

SPEND TIME PROPORTIONAL TO POTENTIAL GAIN

See that the time you expend on each function for which you are responsible is proportional to the potential gain (or loss) from that function. You would not want to spend 20 per cent of your time, for example, interviewing vendors when the purchases you make only amount to 5 per cent of the budget for your operations. Most of the cost of operating an organization is in wages and salaries, which means that the greatest portion of your time should be devoted to working with your subordinates; failure to do so is one of the most common errors in management. (Take the phrase "working with" literally.)

A useful memory aid in this respect is the acrostic "TIDY":

Time
Invested
should be proportional to
Dollar
Yield

Whether you are a salesman, a store manager, an engineer or a teacher, you can do better by keeping your own work "TIDY."

AVOID CONTINUING ACKNOWLEDGMENTS

One can often avoid a continuing correspondence by using the expression "no answer required" or "no answer expected," as the case may be. This may be printed on certain forms or written as a postscript to correspondence. Otherwise, merely as a matter of courtesy, people will acknowledge your communication. Sometimes we even get to the point of acknowledging achknowledgements!

PLAN YOUR WORK ON A
THREE-BY-FIVE CARD

For daily planning, before you leave the office each evening, list the important jobs to be done the following day on a three-by-five card, preferably in the order of priority. In addition to providing a "target," it will feed material into your subconscious for overnight "digesting." But be careful—a common failing is to give priority (both in sequence and in time allocation) to those projects which are of personal interest or are "fun."

For Dennis Horner, branch manager of a department store, tomorrow's card might read like this:

1. Fill vacancy in housewares department.
2. Devise sale for overstock in garden department.
3. Have stained wall repainted.
4. Why are book sales off?
5. See Joe B.—needs a boost.
6. Get started on monthly report; include photos of renovated areas.

He'll be better able to handle these problems once he has listed them like this, in advance.

Summary

Special techniques can be applied to saving time on individual aspects of your work:

Write your answer directly on the letter received.
Conduct a meeting with no chairs in the room.
Try a brain-storming session.
Use post cards for repetitive correspondence.
Make use of your subconscious mind.
Use special correspondence devices.
Reduce the number of report copies.
Utilize the advantages of color-coding.
Prepare an advance agenda for a meeting.
Put down your thoughts in writing.
Make proper use of the dictating machine.
Consider talking faster.
Advertise your buying as well as selling.
Provide callers and visitors with literature.
See that the time you spend is proportional to the potential gain.
Avoid continuing acknowledgements.
Plan tomorrow's work on a three-by-five card.

14

USE PERSONAL MANAGEMENT AIDS

Go, sir, gallop, and don't forget that the world was made in six days. You can ask me for anything you like, except time.
——Napoleon Bonaparte

If you would manage your time, you would manage yourself. Let's consider some of the devices you can use to make yourself more effective in your work, to get better things done in shorter time.

CONSIDER YOUR PROMISE INVIOLATE

A number of small businesses, both manufacturing and service types, have found the same "secret" of survival and growth in fields which appear to be dominated by giant companies. These small organizations prosper because they treat their customers as they treat their personal friends: each is considered an individual, with individual characteristics; and to each, *every promise made is a promise kept.*

We tend to forget how simple, basic truths have such a profound effect on our futures. The individual, just as his organization, soon develops a reputation for sincerity, honesty and personal concern, and the effect of this reputation is difficult to overstate. Once lost or compromised, it is very difficult to regain.

MAKE A LIST OF YOUR SUCCESSES

Make a list of your successes. Review that list regularly and add to it when an occasion warrants. Try to identify the conditions that have led to that success, so that they might be capitalized on in the future. Of course, in a similar way, it is possible to review one's failures, but this negativism can be self-defeating, as several very good current books tell us. Yet, extraordinarily productive people treasure their mistakes. A *mistake* is transformed into an *experience* where one has learned from it. With each mistake you can decide whether to make a forfeit or an investment.

The good salesman realizes that he is at his best right after he has just made a big sale; that's when his confidence and enthusiasm are at a high point. That's the time, he knows, to tackle that really big, tough prospect! But he can also bolster his drive by reviewing a list of his biggest sales. Take the time, periodically, to remind yourself just what you are capable of doing!

MAKE YOURSELF AVAILABLE

Getting things done, remember, doesn't mean holding yourself incommunicado. It does mean, though, seeing people about things that count and spending no more time than the problem deserves.

A friend came to me with a problem recently. He said,

"I've really got it rough. You see, in my plant, I have a bunch of older people, and although I am rather young, they come to me for advice. And, boy, do they like to talk. But they don't seem to have real bad problems, just little things they want to talk about."

"You mean," I asked, "that the things they want to talk about don't involve their work?"

He answered, "Oh, just sometimes, but not important things. Really, they just like to gab. And it wastes so much of my time that I can't get my work done."

"It's a good sign, of course, that they want to talk to you—at least they trust you and don't dislike you. How is production?"

"It's good, I'd say," he replied. "But I get the feeling sometimes that talking to me is just an excuse to relax. I must spend half of my time just talking. . . ."

"Your problem is to cut down on this time while still giving them the feeling that you want to talk with them. What do you think would happen if you announced that, because of your desire to talk with anyone who wanted an audience while still performing your duties to them as their manager, you would set aside the two hours immediately following the end of the work shift for this purpose?"

"Well," he mused, "I don't think most of them would stay—they want to get home too badly. But if someone had anything important to say, he *would* stay. If it concerned his job, I could pay him for the time, and, of course, I could still see anybody during the day that had something important about the work to say."

"In other words, you'd still be talking with them about the important stuff, but the idle conversation would cease."

"Yes, I think it might work."

We want to be available for controllable periods of time and for constructive ends.

Perhaps you have seen a sign which is in rather common use on office doors: "Must you see me now? If not, please go away!"

The thought is valuable but much too negative. This sign would get more positive response and better results: "Come in! But first, be sure you have defined your problem and have prepared your recommendation for its solution."

MAKE USE OF CODE WORDS

Code words can be helpful under certain conditions. For example, a subordinate may be prone to excitability and emotionalism in meetings, and he may need help trying to correct this situation. You might consider a private code word—such as "features," which is infrequently used but can be worked into almost any situation—to privately remind the person of the situation he is creating.

Or, you might name a code word for yourself, unknown to anyone other than yourself. You may want to be reminded to keep an open mind by reflecting on rigid thinking everytime you hear the words "sure," "positive," or "certain."

You might also consider changing key words whenever they appear. For example, when someone says "never," you mentally substitute "hardly ever" in the same sentence and evaluate the result. You might also change "impossible" to "not likely"; "we know" to "it appears"; "definite" to "probable."

QUESTION ANY UNCHANGED ACTIVITY

If you are looking for items which have a considerable improvement potential, merely make a list of everything that has been done the same way for the last five years—or certainly for the last ten years. Technology and techniques are changing so fast these days that systems five years old are obsolete, or at least obsolescent.

From an equipment standpoint (with weapons as the prime example), only the items on the drawing boards are modern; items which have reached the production stage are already obsolete. (When investigating puchase of a type of equipment, find out what is on the drawing boards in addition to what is on the market!)

REQUIRE THAT RECOMMENDATIONS ACCOMPANY PROBLEMS

Require subordinates to provide their recommendation for the solution of whatever problem they bring. This builds leaders, since problem-solving is of more value to an organization than problem-finding.

Train your people, then, to consider that everything brought to your attention has two parts: the definition of the problem, and their recommendation for its solution. And that if they present you with a defined problem only, they have done half a job. If the problem is brought to you undefined, finally, they have done you *no* service!

Your subordinates, in turn, should use the same technique in developing the skills of the people under them, just as you develop your own skills in using the technique when reporting to your superiors.

PROVIDE A COOLING-OFF PERIOD

If you will hold onto a letter that angered or annoyed you for a day or two before trying to answer it, you will probably be able to prepare a better reply.

Similarly, if you wanted to talk to a subordinate who angered you, it would be best to delay that discussion until you had a chance to calmly consider the man and his problem. In such a case, it's a good idea to remind oneself of the man's good points and his value to your organization.

Rarely, indeed, do men profit in any way from an act in anger.

GET INTERESTED IN PEOPLE'S NAMES

If you are anything other than a person with a very unusual memory, you feel yourself handicapped in your daily work by an inability to remember people's names. You know you could function more effectively as a manager if you could call more people by name; yet you are regularly embarrassed or frustrated because you can't connect their names with their faces.

Although we will discuss memory development in more detail in the next chapter, you can learn people's names easier by considering them as interesting *words*.

Some names denote a former occupation; these derivations can help you remember names such as Cartwright, Baker, Seamster, Carpenter, Mason, Smith, Carrier, Porter, Archer, Cooper, Hunter. A few translations show occupation in other languages such as German: Schneider (tailor), Koch (cook), Eisenschmitt (iron-smith), Fleischbrenner (meat-burner), Gruber (digger).

Many given names have a biblical origin such as Enos (man), Ben (son), Abner (of light), and Dinah (vindicated).

Other names denote a place of origin: Irving Berlin, Julie London, Anatole France.

Ask people how their names were derived and how they prefer to pronounce them. Certainly, no one objects to talking about his name! At a methods-improvement conference in Baltimore some years back, I met a man whose name I shall never forget. His name was Kwekkeboom; he said it was of Danish origin and meant "tree-by-the-brook." But the strangest thing was, he said, that few people ever inquired about his name.

First as well as last names have meaning, of course; there are very few names, relatively, that are synthetic—almost all have a derivation. There are some interesting books on this subject, even listings of possible names for newborns show the meaning. Here's a list of names, along with their actual meanings (why not make such a list of friends' names or names you are trying to remember?):

Name	*Meaning*
Jonathan Wainwright	Jehovah-is-gracious wagon-maker
Andrew Johnson	strong son-of-John
Helen Keller	bright cellar
Margaret Nagel	pearl nail
Paul Nathan	little gift
Aaron Alexander	inspired defender
Mary Peters	bitter stones
Ira Patrick	watchful nobleman

Dinah Hauptman	vindicated captain
Noah Ritter	wandering knight
Calvin Miles	bold soldier
Ruth Burger	beauteous citizen
Abner Cain	luminous possession

DO NOT STRIVE FOR PERFECTION

There is no perfect thing on earth—at least, not materially. We cannot draw a perfectly straight line nor a perfectly round circle, not with the best instruments we can devise. Nothing is really square or flat or smooth. Conceptually, yes, but not in being.

We must substitute approximations, then, in order to use wheels, build buildings, grind lenses. If we held out for the perfect, nothing would ever be built.

This same lesson is valuable in our daily work: if we strive too much for perfection, we cannot complete our work. This is not to say that our work should not be done with care, with craftsmanship, but we must determine what our desirable degree of tolerance is and not waste time and money in going beyond it.

USE THE PSYCHOLOGICAL VALUE
OF DINING

Some of the most effective meetings are those held during, or immediately following, a meal. Are your meetings bogging down in routine? Try a breakfast meeting at a hotel. In addition to group meetings, this is also an effective way to have an interview or a private discussion. One effective manager regularly uses this technique: when differences arise between two department heads, he suggests that they discuss it over breakfast the next morning as the guests of the organization. The next time someone comes to you with a particularly emotional complaint, suggest that he join you for breakfast the next morning. The results of this type of meeting are usually very satisfying.

Many people find, moreover, that sitting in a strange seat in new surroundings can be stimulating, just as travel is stimulating. Thus, bringing people together for meals at a hotel or restaurant, even in their own hometown, can stimulate them to thought. Members of such organizations as Rotary, for example, who have a weekly luncheon meeting, can attest to this.

Of course, like anything else, business meals can be overdone and can begin to waste time if not handled properly.

PEOPLE DON'T FIND THE BEST WAY TO DO THEIR WORK

Do not assume that people find the best way to do a given job, no matter how simple it is, no matter how many repetitions there are. In repetitive assembly operations, for example, it is not uncommon to see a person reach two feet to pick up a small object, and this might be repeated a hundred thousand times or more; yet, that reaching distance might have been shortened to half the distance merely by relocating the container! This is not conjecture—it happens again and again.

In Houston, not too long ago, I was afforded the honor of addressing a building management group. I discussed the fact that workers depend on management for finding better ways of doing their work, and if management defaulted on this responsibility, then the workers usually would go on doing things the way they had been done before—which may well be very inefficient. When the meeting was over, I watched the porter force collecting all the folding chairs. They rolled a cart to the center of the large room, then brought the chairs to it. The average walking distance must have been fifty feet. If one man had moved the cart while the others had placed chairs on it, moving down one side of the room and then back up the other, the average walking distance would have been about five feet, and the job would have been a lot easier and finished sooner.

What a perfect demonstration! These men set out and put away chairs day in, day out. They were working *harder* because management had not helped them by showing the way to work *smarter*.

SEARCH FOR MEANING

One can learn many things from what appear to be commonplace occurrences if one will but search for meaning. At the end of an interview, conference or any sort of unusual occurrence, ask yourself, "What can I learn from this experience?" When you find someone doing something different from you, look to see why.

One of the most successful salesmen I have ever met takes the time to ask himself, at the end of each sales interview, "Now, what did I learn from that call?" And, further, he takes the time to write down that information or evaluation in his daily call book, using phrases such as "seeing the wrong man," "this company is not ready for us," or "needs my product, but afraid to hurt his friends."

See what can be learned from your own contacts;

don't assume that you will learn without actively and consciously seeking to learn.

DO NOT JUMP TO AGREEMENTS

It's just human nature to want to agree to something as quickly as possible; it's the "friendly" thing to do. Yet, the next morning, as the full nature of the agreement finally strikes you, it can be a seriously regretted move. People are particularly prone to jump to agreements at meetings or conferences; that is why it is so desirable to provide an agenda first, as well as good practice to make some important decisions tentative so that they can be completely considered before firming them up.

MAKE CERTAIN THAT AN ERROR DOES NOT RECUR

A repeated error is many times worse than the original error, and this is true whether we are talking about the effect on a customer or on an internal organization.

Make certain that an error does not recur. Do not reprocess the information through the same channels that caused the other error unless you are willing to follow it up.

THINK "YOU MAY BE RIGHT"

Approach every viewpoint which differs with yours with the expression *and* the feeling, "You may be right." Most people immediately assume a defensive posture when confronted with an opinion that differs from theirs. One of the very marks of maturity is the ability to relinquish, even attack, one's own viewpoint.

Although people should give their support to the things they feel are right, they should also hold their minds open to the possibility that they might not be right.

PERSONALIZE YOUR CORRESPONDENCE

A printed letterhead on which words are typed just can't help being cold and impersonal, although the content of the message can soften this to some extent. A good general rule to follow is to write just as you speak so that your personality can come through in your words.

But, beyond this, there are cases—perhaps one or two a day—where it is desirable to personalize a letter; it lets the receiver know that he means something to the writer.

Here are some ways you might enliven your letters:

1. Use ink of a distinctive color, such as purple, brown or green.
2. Use an unusual pen point, such as a lettering pen or a very wide point.
3. Sign the letter with a nickname or just your first initial.
4. Underline, by hand, words or phrases that you feel you want to stress.
5. Put in a handwritten postscript or marginal note.
6. You might even draw in a cartoon, such as a smiling face or a "stick man" to illustrate a point.

7. Attach photos, clippings or other items of interest.

AVOID A CONDITIONED RESPONSE

The first response a person is likely to make to a problem is to react along the lines of his weaknesses. Going back to our characterizations of Chapter Seven, let's see how each man would react to the same problem. Let's say they have been asked to evaluate a proposed new product.

Walter Wordy responds with verbosity. He feels it is his responsibility to fill in all periods of silence with the sound of his voice and all spaces of paper with words of his making. Whatever Walter's feelings about the product, we are going to have a hard time getting at them through all the mass of trimmings.

Paul Paperwork has a simple response: he immediately resorts to forms and reports. The very first thing he thought of when the problem was brought to his attention was a name for the file folder; then, he tried to fill the folder with as much paper as he could find. He may have spent hours, handling dozens of pieces of paper, and has yet to give one real thought to the subject at hand.

Fran Friendly seems unable to spend any real time on this problem because of his preoccupation with visitors and his desire to help Paul Paperwork set up some new forms.

Harry Haphazard launches into the subject without any preparation and interrupts his work on it repeatedly to handle other incoming work. We'll do well to get half an answer from Harry.

Carl Carefree merely puts the work aside; it would interfere with his personal plans for the week.

Barnum N. Bailey considers the problem from the standpoint of making the best impression, of putting on the best show. He festoons his walls with pictures, charts and clever sayings and stacks up his desk with related materials. He makes sure the top piece of each pile is most impressive. When pressed for his final opinion, he will hedge by saying that he had so much to do he couldn't go very deeply into it.

These men didn't respond in their own special ways deliberately or consciously; they did it through habit and through failure to recognize that they are compounding their weaknesses.

I once flew from Hartford to Raleigh; it was unavoidable that I change planes in New York. As I entered the airline waiting area in LaGuardia Terminal, I noticed that most of the people sitting about were of a social minority. I blush to think that my first thoughts were for my personal safety, based on memories of lurid newspaper stories about mob crimes.

I took an inconspicuous seat and began to do some reading.

On looking up, perhaps five minutes later, a remarkable transformation had taken place. The same people were there, but now I saw them as individuals, rather than a group. Here were intelligent, alert, smiling faces. I later learned that they were a selected group of college students taking a special field trip.

I had made the mistake of judging a whole thing by a comparison with a selected (but rare) whole thing of similar outward appearance and not considering it as a collection of unique parts, or even as a unique whole in itself.

There are many ways to make thinking mistakes.

This one was in what we might call "group typing," a conditioned response where an outward similarity gives us a false impression of complete similarity.

When you are asked to solve a problem, reserve your statement of opinion until you have been able to put aside any emotional reaction the problem may have brought out and until you have suppressed your own conditioned response to the point where you are able to provide an analytical approach.

SUMMARY

These techniques can help you to make your work more effective:

Consider your promise inviolate.
Make a list of your successes.
Make yourself available.
Make use of code words.
Question any activity which has not changed in five years.
Require subordinates to submit recommendations with problems.
Provide a cooling-off period.
Get interested in people's names.
Do not strive for perfection.
Use the psychological value of dining.
Do not assume that people find the best way to do a job.
Search for meaning.
Do not jump to agreements.
Make certain that an error does not recur.
Think: "you may be right."
Personalize your correspondence.
Avoid a conditioned response.

15

EXPAND
YOUR HORIZONS

*So long as a man imagines that he cannot do this
or that, so long is he determined not to do it; and
consequently, so long it is impossible to him that
he should do it.*

—SPINOZA

Up to this point, we have concerned ourselves with how a
person, such as yourself, can get more done. But you, as a
human being, are incomplete. We all have voids, spaces,
gaps in our make-ups, aside from being much *smaller* persons than we might be otherwise.

If you can get more done as you are, how much more
could you get done if you were a bigger, more complete
person? A tantalizing thought!

Many of us have "holes" in our education. Or, if not
in our education, in our understanding. Such a void might
last a lifetime, simply through fear of failure of an attempt
to fill it.

Having had an engineering education, and concentrating most of my reading on military history, science-fiction,
science and technology, I once knew nothing whatever
about mythology. And yet, mythological references occur

very frequently. But for many years I put off reading any-thing on this subject; perhaps it was a fear of being unable to remember so many names! Anniversaries and holidays are good times to get things started, and on one Thanks-giving Day I determined to study mythology. It was fasci-nating! And valuable, since, of course, the subject is very stimulating to the spirit and intellect.

Similarly, I knew I could never fully appreciate music until I had learned to play a difficult instrument. On my thirtieth birthday, I took up the violin, which has since rewarded me with a much richer musical experience.

Think over *your* range of experience and education. Are there subjects which leave you incomplete? Choose an occasion—the next holiday or your next birthday or anni-versary—and dig into that subject. Some people have even become experts in fields which they formerly abhorred or have taken up as treasured hobbies things which they were completely afraid of before.

Let me give you another example that had a profound effect on my own life. At the age of thirty-five, I attended a series of talks by that remarkable thinker and artist, Leo Katz. (His three-volume work *Understanding Modern Art* is still the prime reference for that subject; it was printed by the Delphian Society *in 1935*.) He pointed out that schools and techniques of art are a matter of viewpoint and that there can be no right and wrong, no good and bad. Works and artists who were "good" two hundred years ago are often considered "bad" today and vice versa. He so cor-rectly pointed out that almost none of us exhibits any purely creative tendencies after our first one or two years of grade school, due in great part to our archaic educational system —designed to do no more than teach basic mchanisms at an average level and quite unable to cope with individual expression, much less encourage it.

I listened with my mind to Leo Katz and realized that, like others, I had very little interest in art as such. In the generation of time between grade school years, where I was last able to make an uninhibited artistic expression, and that moment, I had not given a single serious thought to art. To *art*, which is the record of man, the chronicle of civilization, the fundamental heritage for the future.

The turning point came one evening in my basement workshop where I had invited Mr. Katz. One of my hobbies is model building, and I had spent a whole year of spare time on a ten-inch whale boat, of which I was very proud. I handed him the one-ounce model. He looked at it.

"You have shown patience and skill in duplicating someone else's creation," he said. "Are you content to be a copier? Why not apply yourself to *creation!*"

He had laid me open as if with a scalpel. I will always be able to look back on that very moment as a turning point in my life. A truth had been given me. To protest that I was incapable of creative effort would be pointless because I had never actually *tried*. And I knew there would be no question of good and bad, of judgment or flattery.

And I began to create—not for showing to others, not for selling, not for competition. Naturally, there was no interest in trying to produce results like someone else had done or in coloring in those ridiculous numbered paintings or going to art school.

It was an exhilarating experience—and still is, and will always be. As God is the creator, so is creating the communing with God, just as destruction is the refutation of God (copying being a sort of limbo). Yes, life is fuller. Things are seen in more detail and with more meaning.

And that spirit of creativity has spilled over into other fields. I never really had a desire to write or speak before that time. It has affected even my thinking mechanisms.

Has science, for example, been one of *your* blind spots? Then, tomorrow, begin your scientific education. Demand it of yourself. Are you without artistic experience? Then start painting, sculpting or constructing tomorrow— and remember, no copying! And why not take up that musical instrument or begin writing or whatever is necessary to fill up those voids in yourself.

The growing corporations are those which carry on a vigorous research and development program. The analogy with individuals is nearly complete. The person that works at his own growth and development is the one that prospers and in whom people are willing to "invest."

Let's consider some of the ways in which people grow.

COMMUNICATION—THE BIG BOTTLENECK

Most unfortunately, the faithful transmitting of ideas and viewpoints from one person to another is not proportional to the number of words used (spoken or written), the language chosen, the size of type or the volume of sound.

And, since management means getting things done through others, we *must* be communicative. It benefits us little to save our own time to do more things if we are then unable to see the fruits of these things because we cannot communicate.

Many observers feel that the very survival of humanity will depend on our ability to learn to communicate. And, apparently, we're going to have to learn this very quickly before we are all obliterated by some "accidental" atomic war. Most people seem to be stressing *education*, but most education is merely the collecting and storing of facts;

we should hope that the future brings us schools and universities devoted to *communication* as well as education.

Much of communication has to do with selling—that is, the developing of a desire in others to take action which you favor. (For our definition of selling, let's ignore transactions on a graft basis, which is stealing, or propaganda for unsound purposes, which is deceit.) Undoubtedly, much of the world considers selling a necessary evil, a part of the capitalistic system that we have to put up with. They also put advertising, one of the facets of selling, in this category. Our inability to consider selling in its true light—as a function of communication—has caused us to ignore it as a subject in our school curricula where it would surely do a great deal of good.

There are some general rules for communicating which can be considered as minimum criteria:

1. Use factual information; do not exaggerate or twist.
2. Appeal to the emotion.
3. Empathize with the person being communicated with.
4. Try to eliminate personality discussions.
5. Handle one subject at a time.
6. State the objective quickly and clearly; repeat it as necessary.
7. Carefully choose the right time, the right place, the right people.
8. Know the language well.
9. Use enthusiasm.
10. Do not be satisfied with majority opinions—sell completely.
11. Let others participate.

With respect to verbal communication, Mortimer Adler well said: "So little conversation, in business or in other aspects of our public life, is effective. It could be made more effective if someone could run meetings and see to it that the talks stuck to the point, that relevance was maintained, that the questions were in good order. . . . Conversing with one another is a function for which we are all too little prepared."

At the root of all communications is the fact that people respond on the basis of personal benefit. Picture the people you're trying to reach with a big red "ME" printed on their foreheads. Further, enlist their aid in your program on the basis of personal gain (of any kind) and *your* project becomes *their* project. And, of course, people support the things they help create.

THERE IS NO SUBSTITUTE FOR READING

Exhaustive surveys give us a picture of the reading habits of America's leaders. The findings are hardly startling. The American Management Association finds a rather direct proportion of a man's position to the amount of reading he does. In another survey of our top corporation leaders, the *Harvard Business Review* concluded that today's top executive is "a self-appointed scholar who has found that, to keep pace with rapid change in growth and knowledge, he must continue to learn and inquire." And since about *half* of all the world's available literature has been published in the last *dozen years,* it was natural to dedicate that study to "those who are trying to drink of the flood of literature without being drowned in it."

Books are a distillation of all man's experiences and ideas; periodicals are condensations and compilations of current material. They are, then, gold mines of information to the hungry mind.

Almost all of us have a great latitude for improving our reading speed, as well as the comprehension of that which we have read. It has been said that we use only about one-fifth of our reading capacity. Most people can *double* their reading speed merely by forcing themselves to read faster; and, interestingly, the better one reads, the easier it becomes, and the better retention one enjoys. There are a number of books and courses available on improving reading speed, of course.

Some criteria for good reading:

1. Make yourself read faster.
2. At the end of the reading, go over in your mind what you have read. Ask yourself, "What did I just learn?" Retention is better when one *thinks* about what has been read rather than actually reading it over again.
3. Use every conceivable occasion for reading. Since you do not know when these occasions will present themselves, always have a book with you. Read in waiting rooms, bath rooms, while in transit, during meals when eating alone or while waiting for something to start. John Wesley, the Methodist leader, did much of his reading on horseback, "having other employment at other times."
4. Try to avoid the consideration of individual *words*—certainly never say them aloud—but rather concentrate on phrases and ideas.
5. It is not always best to start at the beginning and read through to the end. It is often help- ful to look over the chapter headings first

and rush through, or even skip, certain por-
tions of the book that are of no interest or
value to you.

6. Try to put to use what you have read as
   quickly as possible.
7. Concentrate on what is being read.
8. Vary your reading. Follow a book on business
   law with one on the history of the Japanese
   Navy, modern art or the latest novel.

There is no substitute for reading, lots of it. More ideas
can be obtained from reading one worth-while book over
a period of several hours than a month of normal conversation and small talk.

Newspapers are definitely not a good substitute for
good books and magazines. Unfortunately, the daily tab-
loids are becoming more and more sensation- and violence-
oriented.

It's not that we get our ideas from reading but that
we stock our fund of information with building blocks for
our own creations to follow.

If you read less than twenty-five books and fifty magazines a year, you are a literary loafer.

WRITING YOUR WRONGS

There are two good ways to organize your thoughts on
a subject: teach it, or write about it. In either case, you
will write, since you must prepare the material to be taught.

Writing is rigid discipline—it confronts you word by
word as you put it down (or into a dictating machine).

Most of us have much more difficulty in writing than
in speaking. A revelation comes when we first learn to speak

onto paper, to say things in writing as we'd say them to another person. It even helps to imagine that someone else is there. One of the advantages of a dictating machine is that one can actually write by talking. (Soon we will have direct voice transcribers, eliminating the need for an intermediate step.)

For most people, an outline is a great help. And also for most people, writing gets a little easier the more one does it, but it is always a struggle—maybe because we know the typed or printed word is so *permanent!*

Questions are always more difficult to word—and are often more important—than statements. Good teachers rely heavily on the judicious question. The Socratic method, of course, is based on a carefully planned series of questions.

SPEAKING OUT

All of us are required to speak publicly at one time or another. (Speaking differs from conversation in that the listener does not reply. Number does not matter—a speech can be given to one person and a conversation might be held among twenty persons.)

Despite the fact that many books have been written on the subject and that one can take courses in speaking—and despite the fact that there are a few "born speakers"—for most of us, the ability to speak effectively comes only with long practice. Yes, there are certain principles and rules worth following, but the main thing is merely getting used to it so that one can concentrate on the presentation rather than having the mind disturbed by other thoughts.

The great problem in speaking is to hold the attention of the audience. No consideration of your ideas, or action in the direction you suggest, is possible by the audience unless you immediately develop a desire in them to listen. The audience must feel that you are doing something *for* them, rather than *to* them.

Just as people can learn to read faster, so can they learn to improve the tempo of their speech, although it's rather more difficult to do and takes constant practice and attention. Some people will have their speech limited by their inability to think at a faster rate, although most studies indicate that we think at four or five times the rate at which we speak.

It takes some people two or three times longer than others to say the same thing; yet speech rate is more of a habit than anything else, often related to one's tempo of life. A drawl is exasperating to many people who haven't got the time, they feel, to move at quite so slow a pace!

Floyd Gibbons left us a good example of what can be done with rate of speech. He spoke a clear, crisp 217 words per minute. (Most people speak at about 100 words per minute.) It was an exciting experience to hear him talk, and certainly there was no wavering of attention.

Probably the value in attempting to speak faster would not be so much in terms of the actual time saved but in the forced requirement to *think* faster.

There is little need for slang or profanity in speaking —any kind of speaking. A person who punctuates his talk with profane words, slang expressions and trite sayings is announcing to the world: "I am unable to use my native tongue." Although most of us conduct our affairs with only a few hundred different words a day, there are tens of thousands at our disposal. Certainly Churchill, Lincoln, Roosevelt, Franklin and Jefferson found a broad enough range of words to create some of the most powerful sentences ever spoken; profanity would have merely weakened them.

Again, some minimum criteria:

1. Keep it short.
2. Believe in what you are saying. (Otherwise, get someone else to say it.)
3. Make *simplicity* the watchword; don't use fancy jargon.
4. Commune with the audience; look at them and make them look at you.
5. Use visual aids or demonstrations if the subject warrants.
6. Relate stories and experiences.
7. Emphasize with gestures, word speed, tone, silences, surprises.
8. Use humor freely—but make it tasteful.
9. Use relevant—but short—quotations.
10. Don't be afraid to be emotional.

In speaking, the most common mistakes are:

4. Using a monotone without inflection.
2. Falling into repetitive phrases and words.
3. Failure to look at the audience—all of it.
4. Self-consciousness.
5. Failure to use gestures.
6. Rambling.
7. Failing to look an individual in the eye.
8. Talking too quietly—or too loudly.

Most of the world's great social changes have been the result of speeches. And, much of your future will probably depend on changes brought about by your speaking.

MEMORY DEVELOPMENT

No one needs to tell you that a good memory is a helpful tool in getting things done or, if you prefer, in making a success of your life.

But neither should anyone have to tell you that you can improve your memory if you want to.

You already know both these things.

Memory aids can keep you from forgetting things, but a chalkboard, tickler file, note pad or chart will hardly help you to a better memory—they may even hinder you by acting as crutches if you use them for everything.

Exercise the memory, like a muscle. Work at using people's names, remembering dates and information. The memory capacity of the brain is apparently inexhaustible—and the more you use it, the easier it becomes to add still more.

Of course it's all right to use memory systems. Remembering by association, especially ridiculous association, can be very helpful. Try reading Harry Lorayne's *How to Develop a Super-Power Memory* (Frederick Fell, 1957).

James Farley remembered by name just about everyone he ever met; Mozart was able to write down an hour's playing of complicated music after one hearing; Harry Lorayne learns several hundred names in a single demonstration; Toscanini committed the scoring of vast quantities of music to memory, note for note, instrument by instrument. Theodore Nadler has learned by heart the contents of complete encyclopedias.

We don't need to go that far (thank heaven!), but when we consider that, for the average person, the rate of forgetting is 25 per cent after one day and 85 per cent after one week, it becomes clear that we need to do better.

And *can* do better.

HOBBIES

A hobby is not to be considered something that sops up "spare time." Rather, there are many good positive reasons for having avocations.

For some, it is an active relief from tension and pressure. A city editor on a daily newspaper, living with time pressures constantly, might find fishing and ichthyology soothing.

Some people develop hobbies as a reserve source of income which can be turned to in hard times or after retirement. A number of delightful cases exist where the hobbies have become so fruitful that people have given up their regular jobs to make their former hobbies their full-time employment. At that time, one should look for another hobby!

Of course, hobbies are broadening; they often call for travel, meeting new people, research.

Hobbies are also helpful in building self-confidence. An otherwise ordinary person, perhaps a grocer, may be the world's leading expert on the philatelics of nineteenth century Portugal.

There are countless hobbies. And many people have more than one hobby—sometimes half a dozen! There are those people who go from one to another, spending six months or a year on each until they become familiar with it. It would seem best to combine an outdoor hobby, such as golf, hunting or camping, with an indoor hobby such as model railroading, model building or collecting. Collecting seems to have an especially strong hold on many; there seems to be a psychological need for it.

Reading is considered by many to be their hobby, but this shouldn't even be counted; everyone should read.

If you do not have at least two hobbies, you are missing a great deal—and possibly not doing your best in your work because you do not periodically release it and return to it with a certain freshness. Some hobbies can be selected which are entirely apart from a person's vocation but which have real value toward it. For example, a study of military history provides innumerable lessons in management, leadership, psychology and procurement.

GROWING MATURITY

Maturity is not a matter of age—it is a matter of behavior. It is acting like an adult, rather than a child, that makes a person mature; this is what makes it possible for us to have mature teen-agers and immature octogenarians.

Just as children have great difficulty in getting things done, so will immature adults. It will be impossible for anyone to follow most of the suggestions made in this book without having reached a reasonable degree of maturity or, at least, without maturing at the same time.

It is easy to make up definitions of maturity by imagining how a child would react to a situation as compared with an adult.

Maturity, then, is the ability to take failures and setbacks with equanimity; to be unselfish; to play (work) with others; to concentrate on some serious topic for a lengthy period of time; to go beyond merely that which is expected; to be truthful in every sense of the word; to be willing to perform unpleasant tasks without complaint; to make decisions and act on them; to consider the future; to function effectively when alone.

Along with maturity, there often grows an interest in cultural things—literature, theatre, art, as well as history, ethics and politics.

With maturity comes self-confidence—a realistic appraisal of one's abilities, tempered, but not burdened, with a knowledge of one's limitations.

There are many roads to developing self-confidence. Some of these are, strangely, interacting: a person who learns to speak in public is thus able to develop more self-confidence; yet a certain amount of self-confidence is required to learn to be able to speak well in public! The development of a broader vocabulary and the ability to write also develop self-confidence.

There are a number of helpful devices, some of which are used by fledgling salesmen, to overcome problems in self-confidence:

1. Dress well. Good grooming, for men as well as women, can make one feel "like a different person."
2. Carry a hundred dollar bill. This really works! (The cost of carrying a one hundred dollar bill for a year is a few dollars in interest.)
3. Imagine an otherwise overpowering person in an embarrassing position—such as sitting behind his desk in his underwear.
4. Mentally review your greatest successes.
5. Tackle the biggest customers (or problems) after a notable accomplishment.

BE A GOOD SALESMAN

There surely are no formulas for being a good sales-man. Of course, it is usually desirable to have a good appearance, exhibit confidence, be sincere, use enthusiasm, work hard. But people who try to do all these things may not succeed in selling.

I once sat on a committee to select a sales promotion manager for a manufacturing company. We listened to four men in turn, all of whom were the dynamic, extroverted, demonstrative type. Then man number five came in. He behaved as if he were an old friend to each of us, but with respect. He spoke calmly and quietly. As his speaking progressed, and he led us further and deeper into his philosophy of sales promotion, he spoke more and more softly, until we were literally on the edges of our chairs, listening for the next word. He got the job.

Selling has got to fit the personality of the seller. Then, it is mostly a matter of exposure, planning, understanding the product or concept, service and persistence.

We have to sell every day, no matter what type of work we do. We have no choice—we *must* be salesmen; our only choice is whether to be good or bad salesmen.

SUMMARY

All of us are incomplete; we have areas of knowledge, skills and arts that need filling in if we are to fulfill our highest ambitions.

Learn to be a good communicator.
Read voraciously.

Learn how to put your thoughts in written form.
Develop your speaking skills.
Improve your memory.
Broaden your interests with hobbies.
Be sure that, while aging, you are also maturing.
Be a good salesman.

16

STIMULATE YOUR CREATIVITY

The most gladsome thing in the world is that few of us fall very low; the saddest is that, with such capabilities, we seldom rise high.
—JAMES BARRIE

Most people go through their lives without a single creative thought, or, if they do have one, they do not recognize it as such. The innovator is going to be "different," and life is full of ways to inhibit differences. Children in kindergarten may be quite expressive and creative, but as they and their friends grow older, they fall into more rigid patterns, and the creativity is repressed, perhaps never to reappear. Thus, as societies tend toward more sameness and more conformity, so will they tend toward less individual creativity.

THE CREATIVE PROCESS

Let's take a look at some of the things that are known, or suspected, about the creative process.

Although some people do find that they get more ideas

237

at certain times of the day, or certain periods of the year, than at others, idea turnout is not related to the total time spent on a problem, the hour or other conditions. It is true, on the other hand, that some environments seem to spawn creative output, as was undoubtedly true during the famous "Golden Age of Pericles." Currently, the MacDowell Colony in Peterborough, New Hampshire is beneficial in this respect. And, being with stimulating people, people with ideas of their own, can trigger your ideas. There are even some drugs which stimulate creative thought, but they are dangerous to use.

Actually, people who are normally quite creative may go for long periods of time without ideas of any kind and then bounce back dramatically. But during that seemingly fallow time, there may have been a very vigorous gestation in the subconscious mind. The subconscious, as we've already considered, can do a great deal of work for us, if we will only let it. Perhaps you have had the experience, if you are a crossword puzzle fan, of giving up on a puzzle one day, then picking it up the next day and finishing it easily. In the interim, the subconscious had an opportunity to "fill in." The subconscious seems to be able to handle much more complicated material than the conscious mind. The nearest thing to subconscious incubation is conscious concentration. This mood, so essential to the thinker, is often mistaken by others as daydreaming or is called absent-mindedness.

Just as in brainstorming, idea quantity is important for individual creativity. The more ideas, the more likely for you that there may be one good one among them. Sometimes ideas act as chain reactions, and one or two good ideas might trigger an excellent one.

Although inventiveness and creativity do not depend on formal education, neither the duration of the education nor

its type, it is true that schooling does make it more likely
that the idea will emerge in a more immediately useful form
and in more detail.

Ideas are personal things—a part of the person who
gives them birth. Some people can't take criticism of their
ideas, no more than of their person. People who might
otherwise be creative, may remain silent for fear of criticism
of their ideas. A certain amount of self-confidence seems
necessary for one to be able to make his ideas public or
even to be willing to test them out on a few intimate friends.

CREATIVITY MEANS CURIOSITY

One thing we do know for certain: the creative mind
is intensely curious. The bounds of that curiosity seem limitless; it isn't bound to the problem at hand but seems to
concern everything. If there is one trait common to great
inventors and creators, it is that they were all-curious.

To a curious person, a dictionary is one of the most
fascinating things in the world. It is almost impossible to
put one down, because one word leads to another, and the
eye picks up interesting words by accident. Are you willing
to read over a word that you do not know without feeling
an inner insistence that you learn its meaning? Have you
bothered to find out the difference between a meteor and a
meteorite? Between a coccyx and an oryx? Between a goo-
gol and a googolplex? Between paladin, palindrome and
palimpsest?

Are you satisfied to know that Monet and Manet were
both French artists—and nothing more?

Does it astound you that there are people who have
driven an automobile for all of their adult lives without
knowing how one works? That most people do not know

why a ship floats or an airplane flies? Or that literate adults may go for years without reading a single book?

It is the truly curious person who devours information and viewpoints, as a starving animal takes food. For the curious, the mind is always starving.

BRAIN-STORMING

Quite the rage some years back, and still in considerable use but in relative decline, is the practice of "brain-storming." The technique was devleoped in order to eliminate problems typically associated with group idea development: letting personal judgment and negative attitudes destroy new ideas.

There are four basic rules for brain-storming:

1. No criticism—it impedes the formulation of ideas.
2. Move freely in any direction.
3. Try for quantity.
4. Try combinations and improvements of ideas.

The brain-storming technique does not short-step the historical method but permits its various steps to be engaged in by more than one person, although most of the time is spent on ideation, the amassing of just as many ideas as possible.

Brain-storming is indeed a stimulating tool for waking up lazy minds, and some types of problems can be attacked successfully with this method, but it should hardly be used as a panacea.

When considering the team approach to problem-solving, it should be remembered that, although thousands of scientists ended up at work on atomic physics, the actual discovery, proof and demonstration of atomic fission was made by just two brilliant people: Otto Hahn and Lise Meitner. The principle of television was developed by a lone man with very limited funds. Typically speaking, if one is willing to trace the source of an idea, even where a team is involved, the idea is found to come from one person, and the team expands on that idea.

Of course, there is no way to "measure" how creative a person is or to supervise the creation of ideas. Some great ideas have come after years of rumination—but in all that time, the person involved would be considered to be doing nothing.

IDEA DEVELOPMENT

In "The Care and Feeding of Ideas," the A. B. Dick Company provided a worthwhile check list for idea development:

1. Can something be modified (Color, Shape, Sound, Odor, Motion, Meaning)?
2. Can something be rearranged (Sequence, Speed, Components, Schedule, Pattern)?
3. Can something be reversed (Put the end at the beginning, turn upside down)?
4. Can something be magnified (Units, Action, Price—Higher, Longer, Thicker, Stronger)?
5. Can something be reduced (Shortened, Condensed, Omitted)?
6. Can something be substituted or alternated (Ingredients, Power, Process, Approach)?

Other methods of stimulating idea development include two-dimensional "bread board" systems, where lists of factors or variables are arranged at right angles to each other and the intersections (sort of like a mileage finder on a road map) taken as new possibilities for combinations. This can be taken further in three dimensions, of course.

Most (but certainly not all) people would like to get more good ideas, invent new devices, create things new to the experience of man. Much has been said and written lately about stimulating creativity, following an almost complete absence of material on the subject before. Formerly, creativity was the domain of the artist, so most people thought, and seemed of little practical significance.

Then came Sputnik and the great technological race between the world's two great powers and the searching look at our educational system that followed.

Unfortunately, much of that fervor has died down (it is resurrected for a short life whenever the Russians move ahead of us again). For us, it is clear that a higher level of creativity and inventiveness must contribute to getting more things done.

The formal steps involved in the creating of ideas are naturally similar to the scientific method:

1. Orientation: Considering the problem.
2. Preparation: Gathering relevant data.
3. Analysis: Breaking down the material collected.
4. Ideation: Listing alternatives.
5. Incubation: Digestion, to invite illumination.
6. Synthesis: Assembling the ideas.
7. Evaluation: Judging the result.

Since it so rarely occurs, no number is given "illumination," that flash of insight or intelligence where, suddenly, as if by divine placement, the idea is in your head where it was not there before. This illumination (represented in cartoons as a flashing light) is not understood at all. Some persons who have had the experience a number of times do believe it is divine; the experience is a thrilling one, certainly, and does inspire awe.

THE CREATOR IS A NONCONFORMIST

One of the reasons that illumination is so difficult to comprehend is that invention does not logically proceed from the data at hand. In the final analysis, the invention is logical only in hindsight; had it been logical before, it would have appeared before. This seems to make it clear that invention cannot come to a perfectly rigid mind. When an invention is made, the principal thing that changes is the attitude of the mind involved.

The innovator, then, is a nonconformist. He cannot think the way other people think, do things the way they do them and yet come up with ideas that are alien to them. If you follow another's directions, you will end up at the same place that person has.

An innovator will be different, but people may be different, of course, without being creative. Arsonists, beatniks and schizophrenics are different, but some may be more destructive than creative. But then, we must be careful not to discriminate on the basis of difference alone— some beatniks are creative and a real asset to our society (whether they want to be or not).

Today's large corporations have highly trained personnel departments that make sure all new employees fall within a rigid circle of conformity; many of the creative people who made our economy what it is today would not be hired by their same companies under today's hiring restrictions! A president of a successful firm—one that he had founded—told me quite candidly that he would be unable to pass the hiring requirements recently set up by his own personnel department. Would many of the great inventions and ideas of the past have been lost if the creative people that had developed them had to work within the strict confines of some of today's larger corporations?

Nothing is sadder, for example, than to see the research, development and engineering departments of our large aerospace corporations at work.

Let's observe Hal Doremus at his desk. He's a design man for the Aero-X Company, and his job is to come up with a new type of pump that will weigh less and be smaller. He sits on row H, desk number sixteen, on the third floor of the R & D Building.

What does he see? Scores of other people "at work," hunching over desks or drawing boards, talking with each other, walking about. What does he hear? The sounds of telephones ringing, files being opened and closed, nervous tappings, coughing, laughter, talking. There are people on all sides of him; in no direction can he see outside the large room he is in. Hal is really in a sort of prison, both mentally and physically.

His management has made a terrible mistake; they have assumed that weight of numbers will solve their design and research problems. But those numbers, and the conditions imposed on them, have drastically reduced the effectiveness of everyone there. It's true that 90 per cent of all scientists and engineers who have ever lived are now at work and that they have accomplished remarkable things.

But many of the things they have done have been from an improvement or developmental standpoint, and new basic ideas and discoveries have not been forthcoming in proportion to this mass of effort and money.

THE CREATIVE ENVIRONMENT

Better to provide one man the right environment for creativity than to stuff a half a dozen behind desks in a crowded room.

True, each person's requirements for a creative environment would be different, but we can list some factors that generally tend toward higher incidence and quality of expression:

1. Understanding, knowledgeable, hard-working leadership which encourages without inhibiting or criticizing.
2. A complete source of information relative to the problems at hand—library, suppliers' literature, foreign abstracts, other people.
3. Stimulating contacts—other creative people, books, fine arts displays or performances.
4. Quiet, calm, natural surroundings—this would require either a private office or one with not more than a few other people in it—plenty of room "to breathe"; pleasant decor in carefully selected colors; carefully-controlled humidity and temperature; good lighting; large windows overlooking landscaped grounds or natural terrain; good sound-conditioning.
5. Adequate freedom—ability to work on the

grounds rather than in an office, no fixed break or lunch periods, no fixed working hours, liberal dress restrictions.

6. Provision of all necessary materials—drawing boards, various types of papers and forms, clerical assistance, calculator, data processer, communications.

7. Assistance from specialists for consultation and work—mathematicians, machinists, pat-ternmakers, metallurgists, etc.

8. Adequate recognition and compensation.

A dozen carefully selected men under such conditions would probably out-perform a hundred under conditions usually found. They would be paid more and would be happier in their work.

The individual can also take steps, similar to those above, to improve his own environment and perhaps the conditions of the persons working with or under him as well.

In his *How to Use Tact and Skill in Handling People* (Frederick Fell, Inc.), Dr. Paul P. Parker tells us: "The whole world stands in need of men who will use this creative imagination. . . . The country is faced . . . with the necessity of solving hundreds of problems. . . . Select just one of those problems. Go after that problem with the determination that you are going to solve it."

Good advice!

Summary

Although the actual flash of inspiration is an enigma, there is much that can be done to stimulate creativity and innovation.

Creativity can be affected by the environment, time of day, the presence of other personalities and even drugs.

The subconscious mind plays an important, although un-measurable, part.

The creative person is a person who is intensely curious.

Both brain-storming and individual contemplation have their place.

Ideas are fragile—they must be protected.

A check list is helpful in making improvements.

The bread board technique can suggest better combinations.

The creator is a nonconformist.

You can arrange a better environment for innovation.

17

ALL IN A DAY'S WORK

How many a man has dated a new era in his life from the reading of a book.

—Thoreau

A lot of things have been said about what to do, and what not to do, in order to get things done.

But what *should* be expected of a person?

If you need help, the saying goes, go to a busy man. Why? Because if he has attained and held a position of importance, he doubtless knows and uses some of the rules of getting things done. Thus, through good management, he can get still more things done. Some people end up with so much to do that they are forced to use such techniques, whether they were originally inclined to or not.

The strange (and very helpful) thing about people in high positions is that they are easy to talk to and generous in sharing their methods and ideas with others. They certainly have no fear that they are grooming people to take their place because they know that both management *and* leadership abilities are required, the latter particularly entailing many personality traits which cannot be "learned" unless the fundamental material is already there.

248

When a person has been successful, doesn't that mean he has gotten things done? Many people equate success with wealth, but a missionary might be quite successful and have no money whatever while a perfect failure may be a millionaire through inheritance. We in the United States, possibly more than any other people in the world, make the repeated mistake of honoring things other than actual accomplishment.

Let's assume, then, that we were somehow able to determine who were our one hundred most successful men and women on the basis of what they have been able to get done.

Each of these one hundred doers spends his day in a somewhat different way. To begin with, their days will be of different lengths; some of them will put in a fifteen-hour day, and some of them will put in a six-hour day. Although the ability to get things done might be considered as a rate of accomplishment per hour, some people find that their output diminishes sharply after a few hours of intense activity while others move along at a steady rate continuously, to be interrupted only by the need for sleep.

Although there is no exact formula for a manager, any more than there is for a salesman or a writer, we know that these hundred people will have all used the same basic rules, no matter how varied the details. To enter that group, you would have to:

- Develop the determination to succeed
- Define your objectives
- Set big goals for yourself (quality-wise, quantity-wise and time-wise)
- Develop a plan for achieving those goals
- Concentrate your time on the important issues
- Be your own hard taskmaster

- Keep an open mind
- Absorb large quantities of information
- Develop your ability to communicate
- Exercise your creativity

The items concerning leadership and human relations are not always applicable to the subject of getting things done, because we do have individuals engaged in "ivory tower" research, invention, fine arts and the like. But even so, the eschewing of the ability to motivate and get along with people can only be done with the greatest hazard.

With the above generalizations behind us, and a more detailed summary to follow, let's compare a typical working day in the lives of two people: one, a man who knows how to get things done; the other, just an average sort of a guy.

A DAY WITH DON DEXTER

Dexter (a character inspired by one of our clients) actually begins his day's work by preparing for it at the end of the previous day. A few minutes before leaving the office, he makes a list (sometimes mental) of the projects and the items remaining on his desk. He finds it convenient to convert every item of work facing him to a single line on a piece of paper so he will miss nothing and can handle them all conveniently. He arranges this material in order of priority. He then prepares an abbreviated listing to take home for consideration or to feed his subconscious to the point that he will be better prepared for the next morning.

Items which he feels he is unable to get to on the following day will be put in a "tickler file" for some later day on the basis of priority. If the items cannot be handled within the existing month, they are stacked together in a folder for the following month, so that priority may be assigned to them at the beginning of the next month.

When Dexter arrives home, he has left his desk clear. He even believes in keeping his communications equipment in the drawer of his desk, so that absolutely nothing at all remains on top. This has the psychological benefit of giving Don a *finality* to his day's work—tending to clear his mind as well as his desk! Of course, it assures him that there will be no misplacement of data, as well as presenting a surface that can be completely cleaned by the night custodian.

Along these same lines, his office is well organized, without a lot of clutter. He has adequate storage equipment and keeps only items of value, so that it is not necessary to stack papers and other items on window ledges, tops of book cases, file cabinets, or, as some people do, in a box on the floor.

At the ringing of the alarm in the morning, Don is out of bed. Starting the day, to him, is embracing an opportunity rather than facing a chore. He has his personal effects organized, so that bathing and dressing are not a "major production."

Perhaps Dexter takes a commuter train to work; this is where he gets his reading of trade periodicals done, along with other printed material. In his previous job, when he drove to work, he would always tune in the news broadcasts so that he could avoid reading most of the evening newspaper and thereby devote that time to periodicals and literature.

Once at work, he digs in, knowing that the important, difficult work is best done quickly while he is at his peak energy. He saves any especially pleasurable or easy job for "dessert."

Don uses the morning coffee break as an opportunity

to keep up his personal contacts with all levels of personnel throughout his organization; oftentimes, he will skip the afternoon coffee break if he is running behind the schedule he has set for himself that day.

He has made sure that his secretary has screened out unimportant telephone calls and visitors and handled those which remain effectively. He is generous enough to his callers to want to conserve their time as well as his own.

His letters are short, his conversations are short— but he sticks to the point and completes those things that require completion.

At home, he has a choice of two or three varied hobbies, attends an occasional movie with his family (realizing that his time is worth more than the price of admission, he doesn't mind walking out on a poor movie) and attends as many cultural events as possible.

We know pretty much how Don will conduct a day's work. These things go into a year of his time in addition to his job:

> He will enjoy two or three weeks of vacation (liberally interspersed with a number of other things on this list).
>
> If he hasn't obtained a job that requires some travel, he makes certain that he makes at least a few trips a year to conventions, meetings or for other purposes.
>
> He had tried to achieve, during the year, at least a 20 per cent improvement in business responsibility, along with provision for an equal growth the following year. He knows if he exercises the responsibility adequately, then the compensation will come along nat-

urally—or the opportunity to obtain it elsewhere.

He will read a few dozen books.

He reads six magazines regularly, along with
looking at a few others from time to time.

He completes twelve long-term projects, about
one a month. (This is the type most people
never seem to get around to.)

He works with at least two hobbies, one or more
times every month.

He might be pursuing a patent, trademark regis-
tration or entering a contest.

He will give a half-dozen speeches.

He will be an active member of one or two
organizations and financially support a number of others, but he may find time to attend
only a half-dozen meetings a year.

He may enjoy writing and will write several
magazine articles or work on that novel he
has always wanted to do.

He will enjoy an outdoor sport, or perhaps play
a musical instrument.

There is a crisp precision in getting things done. His
day has a crystalline rather than amorphous structure.

Ask Don Dexter what he is working toward, and
he will likely give you an answer in terms of a fixed goal.
And just as naturally, you presume that he will attain it.

A DAY WITH JOHN TRENT

The important thing to bear in mind about the working habits of John Trent (another client-suggested characterization) is that he does not consider himself a time-waster. Quite the contrary, he thinks he is a successful business executive. *As a matter of fact, so do most other people.* It takes a pretty knowledgeable person to discern John's failings in his working habits, although they show up clearly enough in results.

He has been a marginal employee to his corporation ever since he first started on the job. But that's been twenty years, and his company has long since discovered that it has to put up with a preponderance of marginal cases, since there are so few really productive workers available. This, of course, is true in all levels of the company except at the very apex of the organizational pyramid. Thank goodness, John will never get that far. . . .

He puts on quite a show in his office. People are coming in and out all day, telephones are ringing, there are letters and papers and magazines and inter-office correspondence all over the place. His desk is piled high with all sorts of printed matter.

To be sure, he sets priorities, too, but more on the basis of what he feels like he has time for, what will impress whom and the need for "putting out fires."

There's plenty of spare time for John; after all, he doesn't believe in bringing his work home with him. He prides himself in reading the daily newspaper almost from cover to cover. People learn things that way, he tells you. He also finds time for a few of the latest novels each year.

Plenty of spectator sports, socializing, conferences and lots of television.

For him, every day is a complete unit, unrelated to the day (or events) immediately preceding or following.

Perhaps he was involved in this conversation overheard on a plane:

"What do you do for a living?"

"I am an industrial engineer," answered John.

"What do you actually do?"

"Well, let's see, now. It's very hard to explain. We deal with men and machines; I guess we try to help turn them into better things. Yes, that's it, we try to help people improve things."

"Where are you going now?"

"I'm going to a job interview."

Without even a clear understanding of his own profession, our acquaintance has as limited a future as his definition—which fits a junk dealer better than himself.

And what is John Trent working toward? He answers, "retirement."

THE CORPORATION

What is a corporation? It might be considered a many-headed animal with an extraordinary appetite. Habitat: capitalistic areas of the world. Occurs in a wide size range and cannibalistic at times. Always hungry and must feed constantly to live, regardless of size. Asks its servants regularly, "What have you done for me lately?" Very kind to those who find new feeding grounds or devote themselves to its well-being; discards those who behave otherwise, unless it has grown old and fat.

Too many people, like John Trent perhaps, look upon the corporation as a benevolent protector. They expect to be paid in advance for their work, considering salary a pre-payment, a retainer, for the services that they may provide later.

But some people, like Don Dexter, look at it more realistically. He considers his salary is a payment for services previously rendered. He knows that he can always earn more money elsewhere but that on the other hand he can be replaced for less money than he is now earning. He accepts these facts, doesn't brood on them and goes right on working.

Dexter strives to earn more responsibility and authority and lets them bring him more money as a reward for his services. He considers every earnings level as something to outgrow through ever-increasing productivity. He knows that earnings are not (or should not be) plateaus which, once attained, are held without further effort. As a matter of fact, he agrees with the corporate trend toward salary reductions for failure to grow. After all, it is results, not efforts, that count.

He guards against feelings of self-importance, realizing that complacency is not compatible with growth. The day a man feels that he has become irreplaceable can be the same day on which his boss decides to fire him.

Don knows, as most of us know, that there is no alternative to growth but failure.

A CASE OF PRACTICE MANAGEMENT

I had the pleasure, recently, of working with one of the country's most successful independent insurance agents.

Although a lifetime member of the Million Dollar Round Table and writing several million dollars of insurance annually, he was concerned about the future.

He confided in me that, as he grew older, he found himself less frequently able to put in the twelve hours a day, seven days a week that he had regularly done before. Since the larger part of his time was spent in his office, he wisely felt that more effective management of his desk time would permit him to continue to spend the same weekly hours with his clients and prospects, while shortening his total work week.

We sat down in his office for a talk. I first pointed out that very long working hours can hide a number of ineffective methods that do not really become apparent until one can no longer put in those hours. An effective device, in such a case, is to imagine the result of one's doctor insisting on a forty-hour work week for health reasons. What would one do? Once this is determined, the *important* things will be seen to, so why wait until one gets six to make the change?

As we talked, I warned Mr. Denton (as we will call him) that his first reactions to my suggestions might be defensive but that he should no more resist relying on me for information on time management than I should feel apologetic about coming to him for advice on estate planning. I further told him that much of the return on his investment in my time (I thought three days should do it) would come from my acting as an alter-conscience, stimulating him to immediate action on things that he had known, or thought, to be good techniques but had simply never done anything about. He accepted all this graciously in conversation, and I saw to it that we moved so quickly thereafter that he had no time to marshall any latent forces of resistance.

Once the stage has been set for change, it is best to move quickly. The watchword is *action*.

Mr. Denton's desk and other surfaces in his office were piled high with papers and literature of all types, in a general mixture of old and new, important and useless, large and small. He agreed that, with so much material in sight, he never felt that he had control of his paperwork. (This was well demonstrated later on when he came across an important, unopened letter from a college president that was already two weeks old.) He further agreed to follow the "clear desk technique" ruthlessly. This system requires that nothing be on the desk that cannot be handled that day; it relegates all other material to a tickler file. (We actually took time out to go to an office supply company to buy the month and date dividers for the file, so that our momentum would not be lost.)

I asked Mr. Denton to go through every item exposed and to put it in one of these categories:

1. *Active*: this included any item that involved a client or potential client, as well as personal items.
2. *Project*: this concerned work that would be desirable to have done but which was not actually required for daily operations.
3. *Reading*: here we had the books, magazines and newsletters that concerned his fields of interest, which he hoped to read later.
4. *Trash*: I gave his weight in junk as our discard objective (we came close, too!).

We then prepared four locations for all paperwork, one for each category:

1. The tickler file was to contain all active material of small size. The file dividers were marked for days of the month, months of the year, and we also had dividers for each of the next five years.
2. A storage cabinet was cleared and marked for all project material, as well as for active items too bulky for the tickler file. (Where an active item went into the storage cabinet, a single slip of paper relating to it was placed in the tickler file.) The bottom shelf of the cabinet was reserved for samples, forms and other bulky material unrelated to other storage in the office.
3. Two shelves in the bookcase were cleared and marked for "intended reading." This was to include newspaper clippings, catalogs, circulars, books, newsletters, magazines and hobby items.
4. Finally, we brought in a large cardboard box for trash.

We were ready to get to work.

I asked Mr. Denton to go through every single item on his desk (and then in his desk and later in and on other furniture) and determine which of the four categories it was to be placed in. Our objective was to remove from his sight all material that he could not handle that day— and since we would take up the whole day with our work of reorganization, that meant everything!

I particularly impressed on him the importance of being ruthless in discarding things. Whenever he hesitated, I asked him if he would be willing to pay me a dollar in order to keep that item; it usually went into the trash box on that basis.

We came across a large rolled-up calendar which he opened and showed me. It contained a beautiful vacation scene which he said was too pretty to throw away. I noticed that the calendar was four years old, and he admitted that this was the first time he had looked at it since he first rolled it up. He said he had no intention of framing it and no plans of referring to it. Because of its bulk, its storage space would be particularly costly, and I asked him if it would be worth five dollars to him to keep it. He threw it away.

Each of the active and project items required a decision in relative priority. At each impasse, he simply answered the question, "What is the soonest date this can be done?" It was natural to set up too many things too early, but as more items were considered, they caused some reshuffling in the tickler file and thus changing of priorities.

At the end of the day, Mr. Denton said he had never made so many decisions in so short a time! But he felt an immense relief that he had control of his work for the first time in years. His desk was clear; some parts of it hadn't been exposed to the light in months. We had even eliminated duplicate calendars and ash trays, so that all that remained was a calendar pad, ash tray and telephone.

We had made a good beginning that first day. After making an appointment for another day together a few weeks later, I cautioned him to remember that the most important things to do were:

> 1. Refer to the tickler file first thing each day without fail. At the end of the month, distribute the items for the following month by the day.

2. Evaluate all incoming material as we had done the other material; if it should not or could not be handled that same day, it was to go into storage or the tickler file, causing a priority shuffle if necessary.
3. Get into the habit of clearing his desk at the end of each day. Even the things that were to be done the following morning should be put in the tickler.

When I returned for a second day of work with Denton, a few weeks later, I found him to have developed the new techniques as routine habits. He felt these devices had helped him so much that there was hardly anything else to be done and that I might as well go home! He said that his whole mental attitude toward his paperwork had changed now that each day had such a *finality* to it, and again he mentioned the word *relief*.

But I urged him to take two more important steps, and he agreed without knowing what they were.

I had determined to spend this day on dictation. In our first conversation, he had told me that he had tried dictating machines but never felt confident about what he wrote. He said he knew that dictating verbally to his secretary was a waste of time, so he wrote out his letters in longhand, made the necessary corrections and his secretary typed from that. Whenever he wanted anything done, he called her in or wrote out a note.

I first pointed out that his secretary was qualified and compensated as a secretary, but he was doing her work (at a dozen times her salary) and was thus using her simply as a *typist* and file clerk. I pointed out that we must use a system that would give her information faster and let her save him time.

He described his experiences with dictating machines. His first two trials had been with the record-cutting type, and he had punched so many corrections in the guide tape that it looked like a doily. His secretary had to rough everything, he then proofed it, and she made a retyping. This clearly did not save time. Then, a salesman left him a magnetic-type recorder on trial, but he never got the knack of it. He admitted that his earlier bad experiences probably affected him and that he felt distressed, somehow, that the machine showed no physical results of the dictation as the record did, where one could watch the grooves being cut. He also said he didn't prepare an outline for complicated dictation.

I had brought a portable magnetic-belt-type dictator with me, as well as a transcriber for his secretary. We spent the rest of the day in working together with these machines, and by the end of the day he and his secretary were in love with them. He picked up the telephone and ordered a set.

Along with reviewing a booklet prepared by the manufacturer, I also stressed these points:

1. An outline for long or complex dictation is very helpful.
2. His secretary was to be called in only for immediate needs; everything else was to be said to her in the record, just as in conversation.
3. The record identification tapes were to be identified according to priority, and the supporting literature was to be kept with the record.

Further, he was to take his dictating machine with

him in his car; we had obtained an adaptor so it could be plugged into the dashboard. He would dictate any thought that might occur while driving, as well as record impressions and write letters immediately after seeing a prospect or client, while all the data was still fresh in his mind. When he went on trips for a few days at a time, he would mail the records to his secretary, so the letters would be ready for his signature on his return.

After a review, which included the systems set up on our first day, our second day together was over.

Some time later we got together for our third and final day in this basic phase of work and time organization. We concerned ourselves with correspondence, the single largest increment of Mr. Denton's time involvement. We had already set the scene for this in our work on dictation; now we would finish.

Denton's practice was to write each letter as if it were his first attempt at composition. Some turned out good, some bad, but they were all time-consuming.

The first thing we did was make photostats of his last hundred letters. We then arranged them in stacks according to general type—prospecting for new accounts, follow-ups on previous contacts, letters to clients, answers to inquiries, personal letters to friends, transmittals to the insurors, etc. We then cut each stack with a scissors into individual paragraphs and arranged the paragraphs in logical sequence. Duplicate paragraphs were discarded, and similar paragraphs were combined and rewritten into one good one. Each paragraph was numbered and given a reference title, and from this, a standard letter was written. This letter was longer than a letter should normally be but contained every subject that might arise with some regularity on the subject. A synopsis was then prepared of each letter, and it was this synopsis that Mr. Denton was to dictate from with the complete standard letter at hand to refer to if need be.

For example, the "prospecting" standard letter synopsis looked like this:

PROSPECTING LETTER

Dear .... :
P-1 Referral by our mutual friend (*name*)
P-2 Our earlier meeting (*place, time*)
P-3 Earlier correspondence (*date*)
P-4 Publicity concerning your activities (*publication, activity*)
P-5 The importance of estate planning
P-6 Taxes
P-7 Will
P-8 Why use an independent
P-9 References (*list*)
P-10 Enclosures (*identify*)
P-11 I'll telepone you (*when*)
P-12 I'll call on you if okay (*when*)
Close.................................

Once these standard letters and synopses were complete, with one copy for Denton and another for his secretary, he began to practice his new correspondence. Most letters could be dictated merely using the standard paragraph numbers, while some needed some alteration in the standards or even new paragraphs. (We agreed that after a few weeks of experience, the standard letters should be revised.)

Denton was delighted to find that he could dictate an entire well-written letter in less than a minute. One went like this:

Prospecting letter to Lawrence A. Mabry,
406 Pine Street, City.

Dear Mr. Mabry:
P-1   Ben Smith
P-4   Yesterday's paper, promotion to Assistant
           Manager
P-5
P-8
P-10 "Estate Planning"
P-12 Next Tuesday morning
Cordially yours, Lou Denton

We also discussed handwritten replies on the original routine letter received and letting his secretary compose other routine letters merely on the basis of a few items of data.

Our immediate work together was over. I made it clear to Mr. Denton that there were a large number of time-saving techniques still open to him and that we might go into some of these at some future date but that the important thing for the next several months was to make full use of the three simple devices that would be of most help to him, in his circumstances:

The tickler file
The dictating machine
Standard letters

It was a simple, basic exercise in time management. It was instructive to Mr. Denton to find that so much more could be done with a few simple devices and that he moved much more quickly than he had thought possible, spurred on as he was by his consultant. It was instructive to me as well, for here was a very successful man, with many years of experience, who touched, at times, the techniques that finally helped him so much but was never able to apply them fully without help.

I am sure he would describe my approach to, and understanding of, insurance in very similar terms!

A lawyer, for example, should no more expect to be a methods engineer than a pediatrician should try to fill his own teeth. I expect consulting in practice management to have a big future.

Summary

In order to improve permanently your current level of productivity, and, even more important, to provide a continuous acceleration of productivity, you must make the self-discipline necessary to make *getting more done* the most important thing in your business life for at least a year. True, one-shot or short-term improvement can be made merely by utilizing some gimmick or putting to work one single idea, but this is like a ripple compared with a tide.

With few exceptions, people are basically self-interested (which makes priests, nuns, reformers and zealots exciting people—they have transferred their interest from inward to outward). People do the things they want to do. And they do them with all their might. It has been said that a lion uses every muscle in its body, with all the strength at its command, to catch a tiny mouse. If you want to loaf, you'll loaf with all your might, and nothing will stand in your way. But if you want to get things done, you'll do that with all your might, too, and again nothing will stand in your way.

However, without a reasonable balance between your work and the other even more important aspects of your life—religion, family, friends—your new accomplishments may be devoid of meaning and leave you without a true feeling of fulfillment.

Nor can we exclude hobbies, recreation and other diversions. We need their stimulation, their refreshment, their new perspective, their restrengthening for the attainment of a long-range goal.

Set your goals high, and set them in such a way that you can measure your progress toward their complete attainment. Follow David J. Schwartz's advice in *The Magic of Thinking Big:* If you've decided on an objective that seems reasonable, then *double* it and try for that! He tells us that: "Capacity is a state of mind. How much we do depends on how much we think we can do."

Continually consider obsolete your performance, your productivity. Today's maximums should become tomorrow's minimums. Consider each day's work rate as "obsolescent."

Don't forget that most progress is not regular. There will be slumps, setbacks, stalls. Just don't stop fighting. Study Winston Churchill's career for a perfect example of progress despite shattering reversals.

Be prepared to wage a war. Be ruthless in fighting procrastination, distraction and entreaties from "well-wishers" to abandon your goals. Determine that you will avoid fruitless pleasantries at times when you should be productive.

Try to spot time-wasting habits in yourself and in others. Personify these wasteful traits; recognize a "Walter Wordy" or "Dave Detail" when you come across one—or when you *become* one.

Remind yourself regularly, with any technique or memory device you choose, of both the actual and the potential value of an hour of your time. A daily reminder is hardly too often.

Develop systems of work. Use planning calendars, charts, a chalkboard, a tickler file, priority systems, check lists, memory aids and any "tricks of the trade" that appeal to you.

You must learn to live with, to embrace, change. Getting things done means leaving things in a condition different from that which existed when you started. You cannot get things done without making changes. Since changes are potentially dangerous—we never really know what the outcome may be or how it may affect us as individuals—getting things done takes courage. Develop that courage. There is no such person as a faint-hearted doer.

Associate with doers, thinkers and busy (*really* busy) people. Stimulate your mind through conversation, lectures, attending concerts, going to museums and, above all, by voracious reading.

Believe in the infinite capacity of the human mind and spirit. Believe that you can become successful in politics or learn to play a difficult instrument or make a million dollars or do a day's work in an hour or be an inventor, composer, speaker, writer, entrepreneur. And then you may.

You must keep an open mind. Do not be unduly impressed with what has been done and said before, no matter how many people were involved or how long it endured.

Develop, exercise, your creative capacity. Resurrect that free spirit which, in most people, has been locked up since grade school years.

Improve your tools of communication: listening, conversing, speaking, writing. They are sharpened by careful use.

Don't be misled by overemphasizing formal education, intelligence quotients or "brain power." If there be in the universe a trillion units of truth and understanding, we can credit a genius with perhaps three such units, a dolt with one and you and I with two each. What we know in proportion to what there is to be known constitutes the first step on a walk to a star.

Develop your ability to work with people. Practice empathy. Work with individuals *as* individuals.

Of course, you will want to develop a better memory, and one of the best ways to use it is to call people by name.

There are all kinds of discipline. There is the kind you find in the army and the kind you must use with children. And there is the kind you must use with yourself.

There is no great conspiracy to keep you from doing more, no society organized to restrain you, no natural law to limit your accomplishments.

But there is *you* against you, and your success will be measured against your ability to cope with your habits, your ability to change directions.

No one knows the limits which one man may attain. Many great achievements have been made by "late starters" who showed little sense of direction or unusual abilities earlier.

Are you prepared for the twenty-four priceless hours you will receive—free of charge—tomorrow? How will you use them? Will you fret and worry over a personal expenditure of five dollars, then think nothing of wasting an hour?

Will you say it is too late?

Perhaps the greatest literary work of Western civilization, *Faust,* was completed by Johann Wolfgang von Goethe at the age of eighty-two, just three months before his death.

What treasures, what ideas, what inventions the world would have lost if everybody stopped work at the age of sixty-five! Yet, sixty-five is the magic age when all abilities are supposed to evaporate, leaving the individual fit for nothing but vegetating.

For the creative man, the man who will get things done, no such artificial gates bar his way. Even the approach of death itself is not a deterrent to some.

Diogenes Laertius tells us: "Very late in life, when he was studying geometry, some one said to Lacydes, 'Is it then a time for you to be learning now?' 'If it is not,' he replied, 'when will it be?' "

Will you commit suicide on your abilities to create and perform? Never is it too late to get things done!

With all our marvelous human resources—a reasoning brain, a seemingly limitless capacity for memory, exquisite senses—we are equipped to understand, to use, only a very small fraction of the things around us. We can recognize and apply what we call "normal laws" to conditions that are short-lived and repeat frequently, but what about an occurrence that might recur every thousand years and last a hundred years—or a microsecond? Our senses reel at the concepts of infinity, death, higher dimensions, space—time.

I have been unable to say anything about the forces of religion and mysticism in the creative life simply because I know nothing. I can only *feel* them and wonder. Perhaps you, too, draw strength from these sources.

It has been said that the longest journey begins with but a single step. Make your beginning, be sure you are on solid ground by repetition and review, and maintain a steady acceleration. Associate with doers and thinkers. Make stimulating contacts. Read. Expose yourself to the arts, those distillations of creativity and expression. Work at it. Before long, it will be a habit.

You'll like the results.

A life is a rock dropped into the ocean of time; deeds are the ripples that move outward and live forever. A life without accomplishment is the stone that lies on the bottom, covered with silt and forgotten.

You began Chapter One of this book by reading the title, "You *Can* Get More Done!" Now, you must close the final chapter with the question, *"Will You?"*

WILL YOU?

EPILOGUE

A GENERATION FROM NOW

Our technology is already so relatively advanced that we can almost make inventions to order. There is a need for a "solid" tire with pneumatic properties. We can expect it to be invented. We can also expect a lightweight, long-life battery, practical disposable clothing, voice transcribers, five-sense entertainment, convenient nuclear energy, practical solar power, self-steering "automobiles," cheap desalinization.

Mere extrapolation, further, will indicate what vast changes can be expected in data processing, automation, transportation, medical science, construction, plastics, packaging, agriculture (including farming the oceans), weather prediction and control.

Breakthroughs are possible in such fundamental areas as anti-gravity, wireless transmission of power, independent robots, ion rocket drive and population control.

These changes will create a condition of plenty, and workers may only put in twenty hours a week for twenty years before retiring, to live to an age of one hundred or more!

These mechanistic developments will create a phenomenal business activity, an intense professional specialization and a ruthless competition.

The demand for management skills will be enormous.

The ability to use *time* effectively, to motivate others, to organize systems of complex variables, to sell ideas and concepts, will continue to be our most sought-after business commodity.

But I believe we can expect our most significant changes in fields dealing with other than material things. First, I think people all over the world are yearning for a new morality and, barring a catastrophic nuclear accident or act of insanity, it may come to us in this next generation.

Perhaps this new morality, which might well involve a universal religion, will come about through contact with extraterrestrial civilizations (it is quite possible that we are *already* in such contact!).

And, we are certain to learn more about extrasensory perception. Maybe telepathy will be a common form of communication in the business life of the future.

Certainly, much research will be done in the phenomenon of death, the nature of time and a serious approach to mystical effects. What we learn may shake us.

Almost without fail, past attempts to visualize the future have been on the conservative side by far. For example, around the end of the last century, most "visionaries" expected people to be traveling as much as *fifty* miles per hour by now.

I'm hopeful that the future will bring a more general recognition of the importance of our teachers, artists and intellectuals and that the creative person will be more understood and encouraged.

We can be certain of one thing only: great changes—some predictable and some not—lie ahead. These can move us backwards or forwards, as we will. Our uses of time alone can make this determination.

Personally, I greet the future with optimism, confidence, curiosity—and impatience!